Get Over Yourself!

get over yourself!

How to Get Real, Get Serious, and Get Ready to Find TRUE LOVE

Patti Novak
and Laura Zigman

BALLANTINE BOOKS / NEW YORK

Get Over Yourself! is a work of nonfiction. Some names and identifying details have been changed.

As of press time, the URLs displayed in this book link or refer to existing websites on the Internet. Random House, Inc. is not responsible for, and should not be deemed to endorse or recommend, any website other than its own or any content available on the Internet (including without limitation at any website, blog page, information page) that is not created by Random House.

Published in the United States by Ballantine Books, an imprint of The Random House Publishing Group, a division of Random House, Inc., New York.

BALLANTINE and colophon are registered trademarks of Random House, Inc.

LIBRARY OF CONGRESS CATALOGING-IN-PUBLICATION DATA
Novak, Patti.
Get over yourself! : How to get real, get serious, and get ready to find true love / Patti Novak with Laura Zigman.
   p. cm.
ISBN 978-0-345-51006-8 (hardcover)
1. Man-woman relationships.   2. Mate selection.
   3. Dating (Social customs)   4. Self-esteem.
      I. Zigman, Laura.   II. Title.
         HQ801.N634 2009
      646.7'7—dc22   2008044362

Printed in the United States of America on acid-free paper

www.ballantinebooks.com

2 4 6 8 9 7 5 3 1

FIRST EDITION

Book design by Casey Hampton

To my angelic Jessica

Prologue

My name is Patti Novak and I'm a matchmaker.

I've been matching hearts and bringing people together to help them find love ever since I can remember. Some people can draw, some people can sing, but I can read people. Give me half an hour with someone and I'll find out their background, their love history, and what their issues are, and before you know it I'll be thinking about who I can match them with. If there were actual qualifications for what I do I'd say I have them all:

I have a sixth sense about people.

I'm nosy.

And I'm always on the job.

Here's my résumé:

I started making matches when I was ten because I didn't have boyfriends and I lived vicariously through all my pretty girlfriends, spending the time I wasn't dating solving their problems.

In eighth grade I was voted "Most Likely to Be the Next Ann Landers."

And in high school I fixed up my brother, Jimmy, with my best friend, Jeannie, and they've been married ever since—almost twenty-four years.

Little did I know that my skills would someday come in handy and I'd get paid to tell people what I think and how to fix their problems.

People always want to know how I make matches—they want to know if I use computers or a twenty-page questionnaire, if I went to school to learn how to do it, or if there's a mathematical formula for it.

I don't, I didn't, and there isn't.

I match with my heart as much as with my brain because matching isn't an exact science—and neither is love. So I do what I do best:

I ask a lot of questions.

I use my intuition.

And I listen to what people tell me about who they are and who they want to meet.

Sometimes the most important thing I hear when I'm interviewing a client is what they're not telling me, since that's usually where their problems lie and where we're going to start. That part—the intervention part—comes later, after I've gotten to know them a little better, which usually happens after I've sent them out on a few dates and I start getting some feedback.

Dating isn't just about having things in common.

Dating is about chemistry.

And chemistry is physical.

But chemistry is also emotional.

Which is why I often think of chemistry as being energy that needs to exist between two people in order for something to happen between them.

What chemistry *isn't* is some kind of equation—similar hobbies divided by differences multiplied by number of qualities you're seeking.

I do match clients with things in common, like two people who love golf and whose favorite drink is whiskey, or two vegetarians who would never in a million years vote Republican.

And yet, the fact that you both like water-skiing and stamp collecting and pizza with anchovies won't mean a thing if you can't stand someone's voice or don't get their sense of humor or if there's no spark when you look at them across the table.

But before there can be chemistry and sparks and a table, there has to be something else:

Dates.

At least a first date, if not a second date and a third date.

And yet one of the biggest obstacles people have in finding love is not knowing how to behave—what to say and what not to say, how to act and how not to act—when they're out in public with someone they've just met.

You'd think they'd know not to talk about how they haven't had a date in ten years.

Or how every single one of their past relationships ended because they cheated or were cheated on.

Or that they're still a virgin.

You'd think they'd know that doing shots of tequila on a first date probably won't lead to a second date.

Or that holding their fork like a toothbrush and eating with their hands might be a major turnoff.

But you'd be surprised at what walks through my door. After all the years I've been doing this I'm still amazed at the stories I hear when I debrief my clients about the dates I've sent them out on. Many people have no idea about what they should and shouldn't do to find love. Hopefully, after you read this book, you won't be one of them.

Helping people find love isn't always easy.

The love business is a tough business—it's the only one in the world where the customer is almost never right and it's my job to tell them that. If they're a 3 looking for a 10, if they're one hundred pounds overweight but tell me they don't want to date a woman with curves, if they're forty-five but dressed like they're twenty-five, I'm the one who has to tell them that their expectations are out of whack or that they're going to have to act their age—or at least dress their age.

But the main thing I tell them is that they have to get over themselves.

Sometimes they have big things to get over—a difficult childhood, a bad breakup, a messy divorce.

Sometimes they have smaller things to get over, like the fact that they're not a size 4, or that they're bald, or that while they might love their eighties hair or their fake-and-bake tan or the fifty rock concert T-shirts hanging up in their closet, those things are actually red flags the size of Texas—huge warning signals—to potential dates.

Whatever it is—whether they have to lose the attitude or grow a set or learn to like themselves—they have to be willing to face what they need to face and fix what they need to fix so I can help them move forward.

For the people who have been living in a dream world until they walk into my office—and let's face it, most of them have, otherwise they probably wouldn't be there in the first place—my advice is not going to make them very happy. It is what it is, though: I'm a straight shooter and I don't sugarcoat the truth because sugarcoating the truth won't help them—or you—find the love they're looking for.

I believe that everyone deserves love.

I also believe that if you're willing to do what it takes—to get to your core and figure out who you are and why and to make some important changes—you'll find it.

Finding love isn't about shoes.

It isn't about how flat your stomach is or how much money you make or whether or not you went to a fancy college.

Finding love is about being vulnerable and being true to yourself.

And about being ready for love.

I don't care if you've never been married or if you've been divorced twice, if you live in the middle of a big city or out in the middle of nowhere where God lost his shoe, if you have a smoking hot bod or are covered in chub—you could meet the perfect person tomorrow and if you're not ready for them, it won't work. Because finding love is also about looking your best and acting your best so you can get through a first date without annoying or repelling someone and make it to the next date.

I tell clients in almost every interview that I don't make the rules,

I just follow them. And that one of the most important rules out there is that it takes tough love to find true love.

That's why I do what I do and why I'm writing this book.

Because I can help you. I don't know everything about everything but I do know this: If you take my advice about getting over your past, if you follow my rules about changing your present, if you let me put you through the same process that I put my clients through in my offices—and if you learn a few commonsense tips, what some people call my "Patti-isms"—you'll be ready for true love when you find it.

And you will find it.

Sooner than you think.

—*Patti Novak*

Contents

Introduction

Patti and Laura Get Matched

The first time I saw Patti Novak on television I realized that except for my seven-year-old son in the next room and my husband upstairs watching baseball, certain things hadn't changed since my single days.

I was still home on a Saturday night flipping channels, I was still fascinated by the mysteries of the human heart, and I was still capable of having traumatic flashbacks to the days when I lived in a tiny studio in New York and thought I would probably be alone for the rest of my life.

Patti's first television series, *Confessions of a Matchmaker*, aired over the summer of 2007, almost ten years after my first novel and anthropological pseudoscientific field guide to (human) male behavior, *Animal Husbandry*, was published, and within minutes of watching Patti do her signature "intake" on potential clients and diagnose their "issues," my dormant obsessive curiosity and nosiness were reawakened. They say you never forget how to ride a bicycle, but I maintain you never forget what it feels like to be single.

Like death and taxes, being single is inevitable, a universal experience that everyone has—at least once. Though we may leave this world with a ring on our finger, we come into it alone and without a clue of how to meet someone and get them to like us.

Some people are less dateless and have more of a clue than others, but sadly, I was not one of those people. And while I was not one of those women who aspired to the goal of marriage and a big wedding, I wanted to find love. More than anything in the world, I wanted to find my soul mate.

But finding a soul mate apparently involved dating (I'd read this somewhere), which was a problem, since dating involved leaving your office or your apartment once in a while (not to mention putting your cigarette out) and wearing something other than black—none of which I did very often. Everyone has their own method for dating and finding love, and mine was simple: I was waiting for someone someday to materialize, *Star Trek*–style, and sweep me off my feet.

Needless to say, this never happened.

What did happen for me and for most of the other single women I knew—attractive, successful, funny, cynical women who were just as dateless as I was—were blind dates and fix-ups. Internet dating hadn't quite taken off yet in the early to mid-1990s, so most of us were left at the mercy of our coupled and married friends, hoping that one of them had a boyfriend or a husband who had a brother or a cousin or a son who might be right for us.

This almost never happened, either.

On the odd occasion when we were lucky enough to meet someone we were attracted to and who we connected with—when the planets aligned and a first date turned into a second and sometimes even a third—the relationship would progress in one of two ways: either the guy would turn out to be a bore, or he would turn out to be a charming charismatic narcissist who appeared as if out of thin air and then disappeared almost as quickly with our broken heart.

Between bad blind dates and no dates, and between bores and soul-sucking heart-stealing narcissists, it's understandable why we were all getting discouraged and giving up on the Dating Game: Why bother playing when the odds for winning were so bad? And yet all the nights I stayed home, all the weekends I went to movies or sat in bookstore cafés with my other single girlfriends complaining about how impossible men were and how seemingly nonexistent they were ("The food is terrible, and the portions are so small!"), I couldn't help feeling like I was supposed to be doing something, *anything*—taking a class, going to bars, faking an ailment and going to a doctor—to meet someone.

As I watched Patti—who was being called "America's Toughest Matchmaker"—get her clients ready for their dates and be brutally frank and completely hilarious, I couldn't help feeling that my twenties and thirties would have been so much different and less depressing if Patti had been around to help me. I'm sure if I'd had the courage to sit across the desk from her—and I probably wouldn't have because deep down I'm a big huge scaredy-cat—she would have told me to lose the edge, to stop wearing so much black, and that it was enough already with the chain-smoking.

But more important, I'm sure she would have told me to get over myself—get over the wounds of my childhood and all my broken hearts—instead of sitting around complaining about not meeting anyone or always getting involved with guys who were, for one reason or another, unavailable. Maybe if I did that I'd be happier and less depressed. And maybe if I were happier and less depressed, I would lose the edge and meet someone. Who was available.

And I'm sure she would have been right.

In fact, I know she would have been right. Because a few years after I started doing just that—getting over myself and finally living my life—I felt happier and less depressed and I lost enough of my edge to meet someone. And just like that, after twenty years of cluelessness, I'd found my soul mate.

A few months after blogging about how terrific I thought Patti and her show were, I was surprised to have the opportunity to meet her—on a semi-blind date—and discuss the possibility of writing a book with her, helping to tell her stories and communicate her message about finding love that I'd come to believe in so strongly.

Even though Patti says chemistry isn't just about having things in common, it certainly didn't hurt us. We have a lot in common— we're exactly the same age, we both have one child, and we're both obsessed with figuring people out. But there's one big important personality difference:

I'm a whiner, and Patti isn't.

And getting over yourself and getting over it, whatever "it" is, instead of being a whiner, I think, is the one secret to finding true love—and everything else important in life—that I wished I'd learned from her long ago.

It's also the lesson that Patti is uniquely qualified to teach anyone who wants to finally learn it and save themselves years and years of fruitless dating. Listen to Patti's simple instructions. Get to your core and find out who you are and why and what that has to do with why you've been dating unsuccessfully all this time. Then listen to Patti's commonsense strategies for how to make some important positive changes—and you will be closer to finding true love than ever before.

I learned a lot from Patti during the course of writing this book—about love and life and relationships and happiness—and I also laughed a lot while learning it. Because Patti's message and the voice and spirit with which she delivers it—her wholly unique blend of compassionate and often hilarious tough love—has the power to change your life if you let it.

—*Laura Zigman*

Part One

getting over what?

It Takes Tough Love to Find True Love

Because Anything Worth Having Requires Straight Talk and Hard Work

There is an obsession in our culture with everything being easy.

Losing weight isn't hard, we're told.

It's easy.

There are magic pills, magic surgeries, and magic creams to give you a perfect body overnight.

Making money isn't hard either.

It's easy, too.

There are CDs, books, weekend seminars, and Internet schemes to help you make millions.

There's an assumption that there is a quick fix for everything. No hard work required.

All we need is desire and that easily made money. If we want to be thin, if we want to be rich, if we want to be everything we're not, all we have to do is to pay someone to get what we want.

To all those people who think finding love is easy, I say this:

Get over yourself!

There is no easy fix for finding love.

I wish I could say that reading this book will be easy—that the advice I'm giving and the work you'll need to do is easy to hear and easy to do. That just reading it—just flipping through the pages and maybe laughing at or recognizing yourself or people you've dated in some of the stories I tell—will automatically cure all of your dating problems.

But it won't.

Finding love is a process. And that process isn't easy.

It requires hard work and commitment—a commitment of time and emotional energy—to get your mind, body, and spirit ready for such a big and important change.

Because you have to find yourself before you can find love.

THE FIRST STEP ON THE LOVE MAP

"Finding yourself" might sound like one of those clichés from the seventies, but it's one of the most fundamental and most basic first steps you have to take on the path to finding love.

Because you can't get over yourself if you don't know what you need to get over.

And you won't figure out what you need to get over until you look inside yourself.

As strange as it may sound, a lot of people who come into my office wanting my services have no idea who they are. Who they *really* are, that is. Some might have an idea who they think they are, or who they hope they are, but nine times out of ten the person I'm interviewing is more of a stranger to him- or herself than to me.

That's because they've never really looked at themselves.

Most people have seen glimpses of themselves—the equivalent of separate snapshots of their personality (they're a little too controlling), or their behavior (they drink a little too much or eat a little too much or talk a little too much), or their personal history (that breakup really knocked them down) that capture small pieces of who they are.

But the problem is that those separate snapshots aren't connected.

Most times, people haven't put those separate little pictures of themselves together to form a complete and cohesive total picture of who they are and what they need to work on.

In other words, they don't have the big picture.

Which is where I come in and where this book comes in.

Think of me and my work as being like the navigation system in a car: You tell it where you are and where you want to go and it gives you directions. It shows you your route, step by step, and it also shows you where you are from a bird's-eye view: from above, looking down. It gives you a wide-angle view of the landscape and of where you are in it.

What I do in my office and in this book is similar: I'm helping you get your big picture.

I'm helping you see yourself and your life in its entirety and helping you understand how all of the parts of yourself fit together. I'm helping you look at yourself and view the landscape of your life through a wide-angle lens.

Once you see your big picture, once you see yourself in a completely realistic way—all your good points and all your problematic points, all your successes and all your disappointments—you'll be able to understand the context of your life: where you came from, where you've been, where you are at this exact moment in time.

And once you know all that, once you have your exact coordinates mapped, we'll be able to take you from where you are right now—without love—to where you want to be: on the road to finding love.

FINDING LOVE IS ABOUT THE JOURNEY AS WELL AS THE DESTINATION

When you're someone who gives advice for a living, people often wonder what credentials you have—where or how you've learned what you know, what makes you qualified to tell them what they need to do to improve their lives, and who you think you are to say they need to start doing things differently than they've been doing them.

So when someone asks me that (and I'm assuming that at least a few of you might be thinking those same thoughts as you read this book) I'm always very honest about the fact that the way I've learned what I've learned is through living my life—getting through the difficult and painful moments, the moments of sadness and loss and struggle—and making it to the other side.

What I haven't learned from my own direct experience I've learned from the thousands of clients I've worked with, by hearing their stories and their thoughts and their feelings that they've been brave enough to share with me about the hard times they've been through and how they survived them.

A lot of what I tell people isn't new.

It isn't earth-shattering or complicated or particularly complex.

The advice I give people about finding love is based on the real-life education I've had over years of hearing about and talking about and looking at relationships and chemistry and human connection and compatibility.

It's also based on how I've navigated through the tough times in my own life—sometimes skillfully, sometimes not so skillfully, sometimes blindly, sometimes following only my strong but intangible gut feelings and the dim flickering light deep inside myself that was always just bright enough to illuminate my path before I completely lost my way.

Like so many of you readers, I've gone through some rough patches.

Like living with severe epilepsy for twenty-two years, and all the shame and embarrassment and isolation that went along with it until I had a stereotactic craniotomy (brain surgery) at the age of thirty-one to correct it.

Like leaving my marriage after seventeen years.

Like losing my dad a few years ago—the charismatic and completely original Buffalo Streets Commissioner James Lindner, who always called me Patti Ann and who I adored, and who told me when I first became a matchmaker that I'd finally found a job where I could use my mouth.

Like having my daughter diagnosed at five weeks old with a very rare infant eye cancer, retinoblastoma, and watching her endure several eye surgeries over the years.

Like spending most of my life struggling to make ends meet.

And like finally finding true love and learning firsthand how facing your demons and getting to your core and healing your soul can lead to such powerful change.

So trust me when I say that anything worth having requires hard work.

Think about all the things you've worked for—a high school diploma, a college degree, a demanding job or interesting career, a hot body—and then think about how you were usually so busy achieving your goal that you barely had time to think about how hard you were working. Sometimes working for what you want feels really good—it gives you a goal, and a sense of purpose, and a feeling of accomplishment when you finally get there.

Love is worth having.

And finding it requires hard work.

But that doesn't have to be a bad thing. In fact, it can be a good thing.

Self-discovery, while scary for some people and uncomfortable for others, doesn't have to be a negative experience. It doesn't have to fill you with dread about what you will find inside yourself when you finally get in there with a crowbar and a headlamp and start looking around.

Figuring out who you are and why can be a very positive experience—it can reward you with a huge sense of relief at finally knowing and understanding yourself in ways you've never known and understood yourself before, and it can give you renewed hope for the future.

All the work you're going to do—all the time and energy you're going to put into getting to your core and getting over yourself—is going to pay off.

Because it will help you find the love you want—and keep it— just the way it helped me.

TOUGH LOVE INTERVIEW = "INTERVENTION"

Some people tell you what you want to hear.

I tell you what you need to hear.

In fact, I often say that I tell clients what their friends won't tell them. Which is why I can usually help them much more than their friends can.

The process of finding love requires that you be grounded in reality, and in order to be grounded in reality you need to be confronted with reality. You need to arrive at a point where you are willing to hear things about yourself you may not want to hear, or accept things about yourself that you haven't wanted to accept.

Maybe what you don't want to hear is that you're turning men off because you've been single so long and have become so self-sufficient that you're communicating the message that you don't really need a man.

Maybe what you don't want to hear is that when you drink a little too much you party a little too much and when you drink and party a little too much you sleep with people you shouldn't.

Maybe what you don't want to hear is that even though you're happy with yourself at the size and weight you are, there are very few men in the world willing to consider dating larger women.

Maybe what you don't want to hear is that you need to get over yourself because women don't find your party-boy behavior that attractive now that you're over forty.

One of the quickest and surest ways to get over yourself is to have an intervention. Most interventions, of course, involve being surrounded by friends and family who have gathered and sat you down to tell you all the things they've never told you in order to help you get better. And interventions are most often about helping a loved one stop using drugs or abusing alcohol. But in my business—the love business—it's to help someone stop doing all the things that have made them unsuccessful daters.

When I interview clients for the first time—when they come to my office to see if they want my matchmaking services and I see if I want to work with them—I basically perform an intervention. There aren't any other people in the room besides the two of us— just me and my client—but the one-on-one intervention I perform is just as intensive a session and as effective at getting them to start understanding their behavior and issues, and seeing how and why those behaviors and issues have been adversely affecting their ability to find—and keep—love.

An intervention is the ultimate act of tough love—an approach designed to get someone to become aware of important issues in their life in the shortest amount of time. While interventions aren't a substitute for long-term therapy or counseling, they're a great tool for a matchmaker like me to use. My intervention-style interview cuts to the chase and gets as close to a new client's core as possible.

Because I don't beat around the bush.

I say it like it is and sometimes the things I say aren't all that easy to hear.

Which brings us back again to the false notion that things are supposed to be easy.

The things I say may not be easy to hear, but I truly believe, if a client listens to me—really listens—and, more important, if a client is willing to hear what I'm saying and absorb it into their core, they're going to experience huge changes in their life.

They're going to understand the small things they're doing wrong and their larger problematic behaviors, and they're going to understand some of the reasons why they do them.

And they're going to see that with that understanding and self-knowledge comes growth, because I give them the tools to help them move forward, past their pasts, and into their future.

HOW TO TAKE MY STRAIGHT TALK

One of the reasons people avoid themselves—avoid their cores and avoid a true and deep understanding of themselves—is because they're afraid: They're afraid of finding out what's hiding under all their rocks, what's lurking in all their dark corners.

Many of the clients I've dealt with are afraid of this very thing—and yet they've managed to overcome some of that fear when they make the decision to see me. At some point they've all realized that it's harder and more painful to keep ignoring themselves—their loneliness, their unfulfilled need for love—than to just suck it up and face whatever it is they've spent years and untold energy trying to ignore.

Many people are afraid of the emotions they're going to feel when they start thinking or talking about the things that have hurt them in the past—difficult childhoods or difficult breakups, or any events and disappointments that have hurt them so much that they

shut down emotionally and sometimes physically, too. They think if
they can just push these unpleasant thoughts and memories away,
maybe they'll almost forget they ever even happened.

To which I say: *Get over it, whatever "it" is, and get over yourself!*

Repressing painful parts of your life or ignoring major disappointments won't serve you well in the long run. Those things, if ignored, only fester in your core and leave you unwell. Unresolved
issues from past relationships—anger or sadness due to painful
losses—will eventually catch up with you in ways that will make it
increasingly difficult for you to have positive and healthy relationships. Many of the clients coming to me (and many of the people
reading this book, I suspect) are looking for help for this very reason.

Some people are afraid to hear what I have to tell them because
they're afraid they won't know how to help themselves. Maybe shyness is their biggest problem and what's kept them alone for most of
their lives, or maybe it's pathological pickiness, or party-boy behavior, but what are they supposed to do with that information? How
are they supposed to figure out what to talk about on a date or learn
basic dating skills? How are they supposed to learn to be less picky
and more accepting, or how to keep their pants on? How are they
supposed to feel hopeful about their future when they are overwhelmed by their shortcomings and failures?

Other people aren't afraid of what they're going to hear—they
just don't really want to hear why they're unsuccessful daters because they're too afraid to fix what needs to be fixed and change
what needs to be changed. Personal accountability and taking responsibility for your own life and the decisions you've made are
nonnegotiable terms for me when it comes to helping clients, and
anyone who's not willing to do that—to own up to their mistakes
and their role in where they are and where they've been over the
course of their life—is someone I can't help and will probably fire.
Because people who are too fearful to help themselves won't be able
to do what it takes to find love—and keep love—down the road.

Don't let your fear rule you because if you do, you're in for a
long, difficult, and sad journey. Whatever you've been afraid of,
whatever reasons you've had for avoiding your core this long, I

hope as you continue to read you'll start to see that hearing and accepting the truth about yourself, while certainly tough at first, is ultimately a great relief. Because most of the time, what most people come to understand about themselves is never as bad as they think it's going to be.

And most of the time, people feel a huge sense of relief when they face themselves. They can finally stop running away from themselves and finally start moving toward answers to questions they never even knew they had: how to date, how to find love, and how to keep love.

THE DIFFERENCE BETWEEN BLAMING AND
TAKING RESPONSIBILITY FOR YOURSELF

People who are unfamiliar with my approach—my tough-love-to-find-true-love approach—might mistakenly assume I'm all about blaming the lonely dateless person for the fact that they are lonely and dateless. How can that be good, they think, when these people have finally summoned the courage and the sense of purpose to come and ask for help in finding love?

For one thing, my method and my approach might be straightforward and honest, but my manner is not harsh. My directness and my no-beating-around-the-bush style is not intended to shame, or wound, or blame: It's intended to help, and I think those who have seen me on TV know that.

Because there's a difference between criticizing yourself and accepting all the blame for why you're alone and haven't found love—and taking responsibility for the choices you've made and the direction you've gone in. And what I'm talking about is the latter—accepting responsibility for the decisions you've made, good and bad, and where those decisions have taken you.

Taking responsibility for the actions in your past regardless of whether or not there were good reasons for making less-than-perfect decisions (there almost always are plenty of good reasons) means you're going to be able to take responsibility for the decision you're making right now—to do what needs to be done to find love—and accept responsibility for the actions you're going to take in the future.

But the message isn't all that matters—the delivery does, too. When I meet with a client and talk to them—when I start to delve into their issues and get a sense of their past from what they're telling me, or not telling me, about their present—I always treat them, first and foremost, with kindness and respect. Being kind and treating people respectfully are probably the two most important aspects of how I work: Without them, I couldn't possibly expect to gain the trust and confidence of my clients.

Kindness and respect aren't just ways to get my clients to open up to me, though of course that's a huge part of the process I've already touched on here in this chapter. They're also the two most fundamental traits people need to find happiness in their lives. That might sound crazy, but kindness toward other people is critical if you want to become a successful dater.

Kindness, or compassion, toward others is something we're going to talk about more in future chapters, since without it you will never be able to accept the imperfections and flaws and shortcomings of the people you meet, and you will have a hard time dating. But treating yourself with kindness—having compassion toward yourself for your own imperfections and flaws and shortcomings—is crucial to the process of getting to your core and getting ready to find love, too.

This, for some reason, is hard for many people to understand.

Most people can understand that they have to be kind to others—or to be kind*er* to others by being more accepting and able to compromise on some of the shallower aspects of dating: wanting a 9 or a 10 and learning to "settle" for a 6 or a 7; wanting someone with a lot of formal education but "settling" for someone who has the equivalent of a master's degree in life experience.

But most people don't get why they need to have compassion toward themselves: why they need to like themselves and be kind to themselves, and why they need, at the very least, to stop hating themselves.

Self-esteem—or, more commonly, the lack of self-esteem—is at the center of almost all the dating problems I see. People who don't value themselves, who don't like themselves, who don't see themselves as worthy of love or happiness or respect tend to go through life without love or happiness or respect. People who don't love themselves can't be loved by others because with dating, just as with other elements of life, what you put out there is what you get in return. If you don't like yourself, if you don't think you deserve to be treated well and to be loved for who you are, you can't expect someone else to like you and treat you well and love you for who you are.

Blaming yourself and getting angry at yourself for your failings—not getting over a painful aspect of your childhood, not getting over a painful relationship, not getting over yourself and the issues that get in the way of finding love—is not only unhelpful, it's not what I believe in. My intention in having an intervention-like approach is not to shame you or make you feel bad about yourself and your life, but to make you see that you can change it.

And that only you can change it.

You can't change why you are the way you are. You can't change the family you came from or the environment you grew up in, and you can't change all the relationships you've had until now. Those relationships—and the reasons why you chose certain people and why you let certain people choose you—are all the product of who you are. And of who you aren't.

Yet.

Instead of berating yourself for the mistakes you've made (and we've all made lots of them) I want you to see that while you need to accept your past and all the "issues" and baggage you have because of it, you can, with some work and determination, change your future.

By understanding your past and leaving it there, you'll be able to get over yourself, move into the future, and find the love you've always wanted.

THE FINAL INGREDIENT IN THE TOUGH LOVE COCKTAIL: HUMOR

One of the reasons I think I've been able to get my clients to hear me—to really hear the help I'm trying to give them—is because I use humor to deliver that help. It feels a little strange, to say the least, to be calling myself funny—usually that's a compliment other people give you, not one you bestow upon yourself—but humor has always been such a big part of my family and my life experience that I can say it without feeling like too much of a bragger.

Humor helps you get over yourself for an obvious reason: If you can laugh at yourself (and even some of the things you've been through), you're going to have a much easier time moving forward and finding love. Being able to have a sense of humor about yourself and the difficulties you've faced and overcome, being able to laugh at your own flaws and shortcomings—and at the disappointments you've suffered—is going to help you in your search for someone special.

Science has shown that laughter is good for you. It can actually physically improve your emotional state of mind and your mood because certain chemicals called endorphins get released into your brain when you laugh. But I don't need science to tell me that laughter is healthy. I'm a big believer in common sense, and common sense tells me that laughing is good for you.

When I'm sitting with someone in my office sometimes I have to tell them why they haven't found love and what they're going to need to stop doing or start doing in order to find it. I have to tell them that they're going to need to stop being so shy or stop interrupting, that they're going to have to update their hair or lose a little weight in order to feel good enough about themselves to get back out there and date. When I'm looking at someone who's vulnerable and who's trying to be as hopeful about their future as possible, I try to deliver my message with as much humor and compassion and kindness as possible. And usually, if I do that, the hardest part of my job is done.

Which means the hardest part of their job lies ahead.

The hardest part for the person sitting in my office and the hardest part of your job as a reader of this book is to hear what I'm telling you and accept it. The only way for that to happen is if you believe that I'm telling you the truth, and that the reason I'm telling you the truth is to help you.

Sometimes the truth hurts, but so much more often it helps.

And helping you find love is the reason I'm here.

It's the reason we're both here.

2

Knowing Who You Are

So You Can Eventually Get Over Yourself
and Out of Your Own Way

I know I've said this before, but I'll say it again because it's one of the most important messages in this book:

Before you can find love you have to know who you are.

This might seem obvious—so obvious that you might be wondering why I'm going to keep repeating it—but you'd be surprised how many people don't know who they are. Lots of the clients who come to see me have problems directly related to the fact that they have no real clue about who they are and how they come across to other people.

And I suspect that if you're reading this book because you've had trouble finding love, you're one of those people, too.

Much has been made over the years in popular culture and the self-help industry on television, in books, and in our schools about self-image: about how important it is for people to have a positive self-image to have a healthier approach to living. Self-esteem is directly related to self-image, and we all know now, probably more than we did in past generations, how incredibly important it is—especially for children—to have a positive feeling about themselves.

Liking yourself, feeling valued for who you are—and accepted for who you're not—is what self-esteem is all about, and having strong self-esteem is one of the most important requirements for a healthy core.

The healthy core that is necessary for finding love.

The healthy core that we're going to get to, more fully, in the next section.

But before you can like yourself for who you are—and accept yourself for who you're not—you have to know who you are. You have to know, and see, and understand yourself.

Your true self.

As I said in the last chapter, most people are afraid to look at themselves too closely. In fact, most of the clients I've worked with have spent much of their lives avoiding themselves, preferring to do almost anything else than to look inside and try to understand themselves better.

Fear is usually the biggest obstacle. Most people are afraid that whatever they're going to find when they turn inward to understand and heal their core is so bad they'd rather not know it's there. So instead of trying to deal with problems and issues and improvements and changes, they shut down. They stop looking at themselves and start looking outward instead—looking to other people for fulfillment, for distraction, for pleasure, for validation.

Denial is another way that people avoid themselves. They might look at themselves, but they don't like what they see, so they decide just to ignore it. Lots of clients who have weight problems or other issues related to appearance are in denial—and while denial allows people to continue functioning in daily life, in the long run it doesn't work. Because denial and self-avoidance keep you from getting over yourself.

Blamers have their own special version of self-avoidance. They look outside themselves for people and circumstances to blame their problems on—but blaming others for everything that's wrong in their lives doesn't help them move forward. It just enables them to keep avoiding themselves and the true issues at their core that get in the way of finding love.

What blamers don't realize is that by avoiding their true selves, they are almost guaranteeing their failure to find love.

Knowing yourself—figuring out who you are and why you are the way you are—doesn't have to be a negative experience.

It can be a great experience.

In fact, getting to your core and seeing yourself fully will help you finally begin to build the life that you want to build: a life that includes love.

I've had clients who have had huge transformations and made huge changes in their lives because they finally saw themselves for who they actually were—adults who had never gotten over their difficult childhoods, maybe, or second-time-arounders who had never gotten over their divorces—not for who they thought they were, or who they were ten or twenty years ago.

And once they saw themselves realistically they were able to figure out the things they liked about themselves and the things they didn't like.

And once they did that, they were able to finally get over themselves and find the love they'd always been looking for.

HONESTY IS THE BEST POLICY

Most of us have been raised hearing the phrase "Honesty is the best policy." It's one of those basic, fundamental truths that guide us through life and help us get through difficult moments because we can see the simple wisdom in that short bit of advice: When in doubt, tell the truth.

Like all good pieces of advice, it's short, sweet, and to the point, which is why most of us, most of the time, follow it.

But usually we assume that this concept of honesty is only relevant in our dealings with others. We're raised to understand that in order to get along with people and to get along in the world, we have to be honest, and straightforward, and truthful.

But what most of us don't understand is that we have to be honest and straightforward and truthful with ourselves, too.

In fact, until we're honest with ourselves—completely honest—it's almost impossible for us to be honest with others.

We may not be intentionally lying to people or intentionally misleading them, but a fundamental lack of self-knowledge almost always causes confusion, miscommunication, and problems in relationships.

Why?

Because when we're not truthful and straightforward and completely honest with ourselves we can't be clear about who we are, why we are the way we are, and what we most want and need to make us feel fulfilled and happy on a deep and long-lasting level. We can't expect to be understood by others when we don't understand ourselves.

Until we have a clear sense of who we are, until we are willing to take a cold hard look at ourselves and identify our weaknesses and problems and to commit to healing ourselves—*at our cores*—we're going to have a lot of problems dealing with other people.

And, obviously, dealing with other people is what we're doing when we're out there dating and trying to find love.

THE INTERVIEW AND INTERVENTION PROCESS

Okay.

So we've talked about my tough love approach.

And we've talked about the importance of being honest with yourself.

Now it's time to put those things together and get started.

This part—the in-depth interview—usually takes place in my office. Those of you who saw *Confessions of a Matchmaker* know that this is where a huge piece of the love-finding process begins:

Sitting across the desk from me and answering my questions.

Truthfully.

Because when people don't answer my questions truthfully, I almost always know it.

Just like on the show, the purpose of the one-on-one in-depth interview I do with clients—and that I'm going to do with you here in this book—is to collect information about yourself. Information that's going to be incredibly useful to you as you move forward in the process of finding love.

Gathering this information and putting it together in a way that makes sense takes time, but more than that it takes a willingness to be as truthful as you can possibly be so that the information you collect is accurate.

During the in-office interview, I collect different kinds of information. Some information is very basic and geared to the here-and-now. For instance, the first and most fundamental question I ask new clients is why they're here (specifically) and what they're looking for in a partner (specifically). Some information I ask for is about their pasts, about their childhoods and family histories as well as their past relationships and breakups. And still more information I try to gather is about the future: what their dreams and hopes are (specifically) when it comes to finding love.

Another important question I ask new clients is why they think they need my help. This sounds a lot like the first question—about why they're here—but it's actually very different. Coming to see me, coming to my office and signing up for my service and sitting across the desk from me, proves that they have made a huge step toward finding love: They've realized that they can't do it themselves and that they need help. This tells me they're serious and ready to get down to work and do what it takes to make some real changes in their thinking and in their behavior.

Some new clients think they just want me to help them meet dateable people—*potentials* is what I call dateable people—and of course, that's what I'm there for. But usually by the end of the first interview they see that they're going to need a different kind of help, too—coaching and guidance to help them with their dating skills and strategies.

These two questions are almost always the first areas where we might disagree.

For example, a client might think they've come to me because they're depressed that all the men they date are jerks, when I think the reason all the men they date are jerks is because the message they're sending—that they don't feel ready for or feel deserving of anything other than jerks—is attracting these jerks.

And because they're letting themselves be picked by these jerks, instead of doing the picking themselves.

A client might think that the reason they agree to date these jerks is because they're lonely, when I think they're lonely because they date all these jerks.

DISCLAIMER: WHAT I'M NOT

I never like to pretend I'm something I'm not, so I just want to make sure we're clear on the obvious:

These questionnaires and quizzes aren't scientific or laboratory-tested.

They're not official personality tests or psychological tests designed by experts.

These questionnaires and quizzes are collections of commonsense questions that I've come up with over the years through my work with thousands of love-challenged clients, which have helped me help them learn more about themselves and become much more in touch with themselves and with reality.

They're also commonsense questions that I've come up with especially for this book, in order to help you do at home for yourself what I do in my office for other people.

Now, if you're looking for tests with some kind of complicated scoring system that's going to tell you just how much you need to get over yourself—a lot, a little, more than anyone I've ever seen—I say this:

Get over yourself!

My tests aren't like that. You're not going to give yourself points or take away points depending on your answers. I'm assuming that if you're reading this book you're here to get over yourself, so who cares about the degree to which you need to get over yourself?

Instead of getting distracted by scores and points and results and ranges, all you're going to do with your answers when you're finished with these tests is this:

Look at them.

Look at them and think about them.

Why?

Because you'd be surprised how many people don't look at and think about the things they do and ways they behave. You'd be surprised how many people get to a point in their lives where they have no idea who they are and what they want. And the reason they got to that point is because they don't look at themselves now and probably haven't for years.

These questionnaires are designed to help you get to know yourself better so that you can eventually get over yourself.

They may not be officially scientific, but I promise you that if you take these tests you'll learn a lot about yourself, and that will help you finally find love.

Or a client might think that the reason they're alone is because they're unattractive when I think the reason they've let themselves go—hurt, sadness, anger, rage—is the real reason they're alone.

But whatever our differences are, we eventually end up on the same page, because usually by the end of that in-depth interview the client leaves my office with a much clearer picture of who they are and why.

Which is what's going to happen in this chapter after you fill out my questionnaires.

You're going to leave this chapter with a much clearer picture of who you are and how you got that way.

(And don't worry: the quizzes and tests aren't graded.)

THE "DO-IT-YOURSELF-AT-HOME GET-TO-KNOW-YOURSELF-SO-YOU-CAN-EVENTUALLY-GET-OVER-YOURSELF" DATING INTERVIEW AND SELF-ASSESSMENT KIT

Part I: Personality Style

The first thing we're going to focus on is your personality—the basics: whether you're introverted or extroverted, adventurous or cautious, pessimistic or optimistic. These starter questions are intended to get a sketch of who you are and what you're like in the broadest strokes.

Notice that some of the questions will focus on how you see yourself while some will focus on how you think others see you. Keep that in mind when you look over your answers at the end of this self-test.

A. Personality Style: General Questions

1. List three things you like least about yourself.

    _____

    _____

    _____

2. List three things you like best about yourself.

    _____

    _____

    _____

3. List three qualities you think are most important for a lasting relationship (i.e., humor, honesty, money, etc).

    _____

    _____

    _____

4. When did you last cry by yourself and why?

    _____

    _____

    _____

5. a. In your family, you are
    __ the only child
    __ the middle child
    __ the oldest child
    of how many?_____

    Do you feel that your position in your family as a child affected your behavior as an adult? If so, explain the strengths and weaknesses it created for you.

    _____

    _____

    b. Your parents
    __ got divorced when you were young
    __ had a rocky and difficult marriage that lasted
    __ had a long and happy marriage

How did your parents' marriage and relationship affect you as a child and how has it affected you as an adult?

_____

_____

6. People who have complimented you say you are:
    a. intelligent and rational
    b. reliable and punctual
    c. romantic and a good talker
    d. spontaneous and full of fun
    e. other _____

7. People who have criticized you have said you are:
    a. controlling, opinionated, or argumentative
    b. stubborn, boring, or unemotional
    c. overemotional, hypersensitive, or needy
    d. too wild, unpredictable, or off-the-wall
    e. other _____

8. If you disagree with someone you're most likely to:
    a. figure out the right thing to do before saying anything
    b. try to forget about it and move on to avoid confrontation
    c. immediately blurt out how you feel and confront the situation head-on
    d. consider possible solutions that would make both of you happy

B. Personality Style: My Most Difficult Qualities

These are the qualities that tend to cause people the most problems. They are the qualities and traits about yourself that you usually try to conceal, especially when meeting someone new. It is important, however, to be aware of your difficult qualities, so we can work to balance them with your great qualities. Check off all the difficult qualities that you see in yourself and make a list of others not on this list so that you can become more aware of them. Keep in mind that we all have difficult qualities and to not have any would be to not be human.

❑ Aggressive   ❑ Angry   ❑ Argumentative

❑ Ambitious   ❑ Anxious   ❑ Arrogant

❑ Awkward   ❑ Gossipy   ❑ Overly sensitive

❑ Bitchy   ❑ Grudge-holding   ❑ Panicky

❑ Braggy   ❑ Hard on myself   ❑ Passive-aggressive

❑ Cheap   ❑ Humorless   ❑ Possessive

❑ Chronically late   ❑ Insecure   ❑ Pushy

❑ Competitive   ❑ Irresponsible   ❑ Quiet/Reserved

❑ Critical   ❑ Jealous   ❑ Self-involved

❑ Defensive   ❑ Judgmental   ❑ Shy

❑ Depressed   ❑ Lazy   ❑ Sloppy

❑ Dishonest   ❑ Materialistic   ❑ Spacey

❑ Disorganized   ❑ Needy   ❑ Standoffish

❑ Distant/Unaffectionate ❑ Negative/Pessimistic   ❑ Suspicious

❑ Drink too much   ❑ Noncommunicative   ❑ Talk too much

❑ Emotionally guarded   ❑ Obsessive   ❑ Unambitious

❑ Fearful   ❑ Opinionated   ❑ Other _____

❑ Full of myself   ❑ Overly dramatic

C. Personality Style: My Best Qualities

These are the qualities you feel good about in yourself. This list will highlight your positive attributes. It is what makes you special and a great catch for someone else. Be as complete and detailed with this list as possible. Go ahead and check off your great qualities and make a note of the ones that are not on this list.

❏ Accepting/Respectful ❏ Fun ❏ Refined

❏ Accomplished ❏ Funny ❏ Relaxed/Laid back

❏ Active/Athletic ❏ Gentle ❏ Religious

❏ Adventurous ❏ Good listener ❏ Responsible

❏ Affectionate ❏ Grateful ❏ Romantic

❏ Articulate ❏ Happy/Cheerful ❏ Secure

❏ Artistic ❏ Honest/Sincere ❏ Sexy

❏ Best friend ❏ Humorous ❏ Spiritual

❏ Caring ❏ Independent ❏ Spontaneous

❏ Committed ❏ Industrious ❏ Spunky

❏ Communicative ❏ Integrity ❏ Strong

❏ Compassionate ❏ Intelligent ❏ Stylish

❏ Contented ❏ Introspective ❏ Successful

❏ Conventional ❏ Kind ❏ Sympathetic

❏ Creative ❏ Leader ❏ Thoughtful

❏ Cultured ❏ Loving ❏ Traditional

❏ Curious ❏ Loyal ❏ Unconventional

❏ Down-to-earth ❏ Nurturing ❏ Understanding

❏ Educated ❏ Old-fashioned ❏ Wise

❏ Empathic ❏ Organized ❏ Other _____

❏ Faithful ❏ Passionate ❏ Other _____

❏ Family-oriented ❏ Positive/Optimistic ❏ Other _____

❏ Feminine/Masculine ❏ Quick-witted

D. Personality Style: Personal Interests

Please circle what interests you most. Be sure to circle only the activities/hobbies you're currently involved in and a few things you want to do in the future.

1. Animals	31. Golf
2. Antiques	32. History
3. Art	33. Home improvement
4. Astrology	34. Horseback riding
5. Astronomy	35. Hunting/Fishing
6. Biking	36. Languages
7. Board games	37. Learning/Education
8. Bowling	38. Marathon running
9. Bridge	39. Martial arts
10. Camping	40. Motor sports
11. Cars	41. Music—jazz
12. Chess	42. Music—classical
13. Children	43. Music—rock
14. Church/Temple involvement	44. Music—blues
	45. Music—independent
15. Collecting	46. Painting
16. Computers	47. Playing sports
17. Conversation	48. Pets—dogs
18. Cooking	49. Pets—cats
19. Crafts	50. Pets—exotic
20. Dancing	51. Philosophy
21. Dining out	52. Photography
22. Eating	53. Piloting aircraft
23. Exercise/Fitness	54. Playing music
24. Extreme sports	55. Politics
25. Family	56. Reading/Books
26. Films/Movies	57. Religion
27. Friendship	58. Running
28. Gardening	59. Science
29. Gambling	60. Science fiction
30. Genealogy	61. Self-improvement

62. Sewing
63. Shopping
64. Snow sports
65. Soap operas
66. Softball
67. Solitude
68. Teaching/coaching
69. Technology
70. Tennis
71. Theater
72. Traveling

73. Vegetarianism
74. Video games
75. Volunteering
76. Watching sports
77. Watching TV
78. Water sports
79. Weight lifting
80. Wildlife
81. Wine tours
82. Woodworking
83. Writing/Blogging

Please list any other interests and hobbies:

_____

_____

_____

Please list the types of music you like:

_____

_____

_____

Please list the types of movies you like:

_____

_____

_____

Please list your favorite things to do on the weekend:

_____

_____

_____

Please list your favorite Web sites:

_____

_____

_____

Please list your favorite foods/cuisines:

_____

_____

_____

Please list your favorite cities:

_____

_____

_____

Please list your favorite TV shows:

_____

_____

_____

Please list your favorite books or authors:

_____

_____

_____

Please list your favorite places in the whole world:

_____

_____

_____

Please list the experiences or events you believe have had the greatest impact on you:

_____

_____

_____

E. Personality Style: Extra Credit Bonus Question

This is one of my favorite questions to ask new clients. Their selection tells me a lot about their personality and what they're truly looking for in a mate.

Imagine you are stranded on an island. Circle the one animal you would want as your companion.

DOG   LION   SHEEP   PEACOCK

End of Part I: Time to Look at Your Answers and Think About What You Wrote

Now that you've finished this section, take a few minutes to look at your answers. Really look at them—your interests, your traits, your likes and dislikes—and try to absorb some of these simple basic facts about yourself. Finding love is all about taking baby steps, so becoming more familiar with this layer of yourself will help you face the other deeper levels of your personality.

RED FLAGS TO WATCH OUT FOR

You've barely checked off any qualities about yourself that you don't like: This is a tip-off that you're not being honest about yourself or that you have trouble taking responsibility for your flaws and mistakes.

You've checked off too many qualities about yourself that you like: Self-esteem is a good thing but no one likes a bragger. Too many check marks here are a sign that you might be more impressed with yourself than other people are.

You've checked off way more great qualities about yourself than bad qualities. This is something I almost always see in my office: a questionnaire with two checkmarks on the worst qualities sheet and ten or twelve or fifteen checkmarks on the best qualities sheet. Go back to the worst qualities sheet and see if you can't get it to look more balanced with the long list of good qualities you think you have.

All your interests and hobbies are solitary ones. You're either lonely or a loner, which means you're going to have to get out more to get over yourself.

■ Your list of favorite Internet sites includes porn sites or more than one dating site and spills over onto another sheet of paper. Get off the computer already so that you can get out more and have an actual life as opposed to just a virtual life!

■ You have circled almost all the items on the personal interests list. No wonder you haven't found love! You're too busy bird watching or taking Chinese cooking classes to have time to date.

■ The spaces for interests and hobbies, favorite activities, favorite music, favorite movies, favorite books, and favorite places are blank. Somebody isn't going to be very interesting on a first date.

■ On my extra credit bonus question you selected the peacock. People who pick the peacock are usually more narcissistic (like Pretty Boys and Center Stagers) than people who pick the other animals. People who select the lion often have issues with control and power.

POSITIVES TO BE REWARDED FOR

- Answering the questions honestly.
- Looking at your answers and taking time to think about them.
- Being willing to learn more about yourself in order to get over yourself, which means continuing on to the next section.

Part II: Dating Style

This section focuses on what your dating style is: which includes everything from the kinds of dates you like and dislike to the kinds of people you're usually attracted to and the ways in which your behavior or issues have affected your dating life up until now. Again, it's important to be as honest as possible so that you'll have a clear sense of who you really are at the end of these exercises.

A. Dating Style: General Questions

1. Looks-wise, I'm usually attracted to people who are
   a. more attractive than me
   b. less attractive than me
   c. about the same

2. a. If I had to rate myself on a scale of 1 to 10—with 1 being the lowest and 10 being the highest—I'm a(n) _____.

   b. Explain your answer

    _____

    _____

3. a. On the same scale of 1 to 10, I'm looking for someone who is a(n) _____.

   b. Explain your answer

    _____

    _____

4. Personality-wise, I'm usually attracted to people who are
   a. more outgoing than I am
   b. less outgoing than I am
   c. about the same

5. On a scale of 1 to 10, I'd rate my sex drive as
   1 2 3 4 5 6 7 8 9 10
     low   *high*

6. Importance of similar religious beliefs in a relationship:
   1 2 3 4 5 6 7 8 9 10
     low   *high*

7. Importance of similar political beliefs in a relationship:
   1 2 3 4 5 6 7 8 9 10
     low   *high*

8. Importance of similar educational background in a relationship:
   1 2 3 4 5 6 7 8 9 10
     low   *high*

9. Importance of similar career and income status in a relationship:
   1 2 3 4 5 6 7 8 9 10
     low   *high*

10. Importance of chemistry or "love at first sight" in a relationship:

1 2 3 4 5 6 7 8 9 10
  low   *high*

11. Importance of sex in a relationship:

1 2 3 4 5 6 7 8 9 10
  low   *high*

12. Importance of similar sex drive in a relationship:

1 2 3 4 5 6 7 8 9 10
  low   *high*

13. Some of the things I've found problematic in past relationships include:

   a. I get bored quickly
   b. I get disappointed easily
   c. I get jealous and possessive
   d. I want commitment and exclusivity when the other person doesn't
   e. I get interested in a third party
   f. I get cheated on
   g. Other _____

14. My strongest dating skills include:

   a. I'm a great conversationalist
   b. I make a great first impression
   c. I'm attractive
   d. I'm a good listener
   e. I have a great sense of humor
   f. Other _____

15. My weakest dating skills include:

   a. I'm shy
   b. I don't talk enough
   c. I talk too much

    d. I don't make a good first impression

    e. I have weight/appearance issues

    f. I'm too picky

    g. Other _____

16. Finish this sentence: I need to get over myself because

_____

_____

_____

17. Please fill in the blanks: In order to get over myself I need to

Stop _____

Start _____

Quit _____

Think about _____

Finally face _____

Fix _____

Change _____

Improve _____

Stop obsessing about _____

Give up _____

Get a grip on _____

Lose the _____

18. I'm a great catch because

_____

_____

_____

19. I generally meet the people I date

    a. online

    b. through friends

    c. through dating services/matchmaking services

    d. in bars and clubs

    e. at church, temple, or through other religious/spiritual groups

    f. at work or on the job

    g. by chance (party, supermarket, bookstore, etc.)

20. The thing(s) I hate most about dating is (are):
    a. potential rejection
    b. feeling disappointed in my date
    c. getting dressed up
    d. going out to restaurants or bars
    e. making conversation
    f. feeling nervous and awkward around someone I've just met
    g. feeling pressured to like someone because I'm tired of being single
    h. feeling afraid that I will embarrass myself or my date by saying something stupid
    i. feeling self-conscious or insecure about my weight or how I look
    j. feeling stressed about spending money
    k. Other _____

21. I find myself in a social situation—other than work—where I have the opportunity to meet "potentials"
    a. often (almost every day)
    b. frequently (a few times a week)
    c. seldom (once a week)
    d. almost never (once a month or less)
    e. Other _____

22. I would describe myself as
    a. outgoing, social, or extroverted
    b. shy, reserved, or introverted
    c. depends on the situation

23. At weddings and parties, I am
    a. the first one on the dance floor and the last one off
    b. willing to dance if asked but not entirely comfortable
    c. wild horses could not drag me out there

24. On a date, I'm most comfortable going to a
    a. bar
    b. bookstore
    c. restaurant

    d. coffeehouse

    e. park or other outdoor area

    f. sporting event

    g. concert or movie

    h. club to go dancing

    i. Other _____

25. On a date, I am least comfortable going to a

    a. bar

    b. bookstore

    c. restaurant

    d. coffeehouse

    e. park or other outdoor area

    f. sporting event

    g. concert or movie

    h. club to go dancing

    i. Other _____

26. When getting to know someone in the early phases of dating, I believe that

    a. you should be completely open and honest about your past because they're just going to find out anyway

    b. you should be honest but not about everything—oversharing is kind of a turnoff

    c. you should save some things for the second and third and fourth dates

    d. don't lie—but don't tell

27. For some reason, I've always found myself attracted to and getting involved with

    a. married men/women

    b. divorced men/women

    c. second-time-arounders with kids

    d. people who are underemployed and need to be financially supported

    e. people who make more money than I do and financially support me

    f. Other _____

28. The reason why most of my relationships have ended and not worked out include
    a. realizing we had nothing in common
    b. arguing/incompatibility
    c. substance abuse issues
    d. temperament/personality differences
    e. boredom
    f. attraction faded
    g. sex life went downhill
    h. jealous of ex (theirs)
    i. feelings for ex (mine)
    j. they didn't get along with my friends/family
    k. I didn't get along with their friends/family
    l. someone cheated
    m. timing issues and commitment issues
    n. mutually agreed to move on
    o. Other _____

29. If I could change one thing about myself magically overnight it would be
    a. my weight
    b. my marital status
    c. my job
    d. my financial status
    e. my personality
    f. my health
    g. Other _____

30. If I could change anything about my appearance it would be
    a. my weight
    b. my legs
    c. my nose
    d. my teeth
    e. my hair
    f. my butt
    g. my height
    h. my wrinkles
    i. Other _____

End of Part II: Time to Look at Your Answers and Think About What You Wrote

Again, now that you've finished this section, take a few minutes to look at your answers. Really look at them: what you think you offer, what you're looking for others to offer you, what types of dating situations you like and dislike, which types of people you're generally attracted to, how you usually meet the people you date. Think about what your answers mean.

Are you surprised by any of your answers?

Do you wish some of your answers were different?

Are you already starting to see things about yourself, your expectations, and what you offer—and don't offer—that might be affecting your dating life?

If any of the questions require more explanation or thought, take some time to expand on your answers in a separate notebook or pad of paper. Those notes, like the ones I take during my intake interviews with clients, will come in handy later as we move further along in the self-discovery process.

RED FLAGS YOU NOTICE

_____

_____

_____

RED FLAGS I THINK YOU SHOULD WATCH OUT FOR:

Most of the questions in this section have no right answers, but a few do have wrong answers:

Question #19: If you answered "f"—that you meet most of the people you date at work—that's a wrong answer. You shouldn't be jeopardizing your job and career and income by using where you work as a hunting ground for dating.

Question #26: If you answered "a" here—that you should be "completely open and honest about your past because they're just going to find out anyway"—that's a wrong answer. Oversharing too soon can be overwhelming and sometimes even inappropriate.

Question #27: If you answered "a"—that you often get involved with married men or women—that's definitely a wrong answer. Not only is it a red flag for commitment issues on your part, it's also a red flag for a lack of integrity.

Question #28: If you answered either "c" or "l"—that most of your relationships have ended because of substance abuse issues or because someone cheated—these are problematic answers. We often go where we came from because it's what we know, so if you're getting involved with people who cheat or who abuse drugs or alcohol, you have to get to the core of why you do that and learn how to stop doing that.

POSITIVES YOU THINK YOU SHOULD BE REWARDED FOR

* _____
* _____
* _____

Part III: Relationship History

We're going to focus on your relationship history in more detail in the next chapter, but for now, answer the following questions to get the basic framework of your romantic past—what type of and how many relationships you've had over the course of your lifetime and especially over the last few years, what difficulties you've gone through in the recent past that have adversely affected your dating life, and what you think your weakest relationship skills are.

Relationship History: General Questions

1. Have you ever been married?
   ❏ Yes
   ❏ No

2. a. Pick a past relationship: When you were most in love as a couple, what three adjectives would your partner have used to describe you?

   b. When you were at your worst as a couple, what three adjectives would your partner have used to describe you?

   c. Now which would you rather be? The person you were at your worst, or the person you were at your best?

3. If you are now divorced, how long ago was your divorce finalized?
   _____ Days
   _____ Months
   _____ Years

4. Do you have children?
   ❑ Yes
   ❑ No
   If yes, how many? _____
   If yes, do they live with you? _____
   If no, why? (It's okay!) _____

5. Which word(s) best describe(s) your relationship and dating history?
   ❑ Successful
   ❑ Rocky
   ❑ Spotty
   ❑ Good
   ❑ Could be better
   ❑ I need help

6. a. Have you ever gone to see a couples or marriage counselor?
   ❑ Yes
   ❑ No
   b. If yes, what did the counselor say to you about your issues?
   _____

7. How many relationships—longer than eight months and exclusive—have you had?
   Over the course of your lifetime _____
   In the past ten years _____

In the last five years _____

8. How many relationships that were shorter than six months have you had?
   Over the course of your lifetime _____
   In the past ten years _____
   In the last five years _____

9. What has your dating life been like over the last year?
   ❑ A little too much action (Explain _____)
   ❑ Spotty
   ❑ Good but not going anywhere
   ❑ Nonexistent

10. To what do you attribute the problematic state of your love life?
    ❑ Busy with kids and job
    ❑ Still getting over a breakup
    ❑ Your weight and appearance
    ❑ Depressed over the death of a loved one
    ❑ Other _____

11. How many dates do you usually wait before deciding to become sexually active with someone?
    ❑ 1–3
    ❑ 4–8
    ❑ 9–15
    ❑ I don't usually wait

12. Which, if any, of the following stressful situations have you been in over the last three to five years?
    ❑ Serious illness
    ❑ Serious illness of a loved one
    ❑ Death of a parent
    ❑ Death of a spouse
    ❑ Separation
    ❑ Divorce
    ❑ Lost or changed job
    ❑ Substance abuse
    ❑ Someone else's substance abuse
    ❑ Problems with children
    ❑ Financial problems
    ❑ Depression or other emotional problem
    ❑ Moved
    ❑ Other _____

13. Pick the issues you think you most need to focus on in order to get over yourself and find love and the statements that are most accurate:

❑ Trust issues   ❑ Too picky

❑ Control issues   ❑ Not picky enough

❑ Fidelity/cheating issues   ❑ Too easy

❑ Problems with drinking   ❑ Too uptight

❑ Having trouble meeting   ❑ Acting my age
   people

❑ Spending too much time
   online

❑ I can meet people but have trouble getting asked out

❑ I get asked out but have trouble getting past the first date

❑ I get past the first date but can't get past the second date

❑ I get past the second date but almost never have a third date

❑ Other

_____

_____

End of Part III: Time to Look at Your Answers and Think About What You Wrote

Now that you've come to the end of the third section—and the entire test—take a break and think about the information you've just gathered about yourself. As you did at the end of the previous sections, take a few minutes to look at your answers to the questions about your relationship history, and once again consider what they mean.

Are you surprised by any of your answers?

Embarrassed by any of your answers?

Do your answers seem to confirm your previous thoughts about yourself—say, that most of your relationship problems are caused by outside sources and other people ("it's them, not me")?

Or do your answers hint at the idea that you might actually have something to do with your relationship problems? That the choices you've made and the expectations you have—too low or too high—have led you into relationships that haven't been good for you or that haven't worked out?

If you're starting to see your role in things—then you're doing the tests right and you're being honest with yourself.

And that means you're going to have a lot better chance of getting over yourself by the end of the book and successfully finding love.

RED FLAGS TO BE AWARE OF

You have no long-term relationships listed.

You have no relationships of any kind listed.

Your list of short-term relationships had to be continued onto a separate sheet of paper.

You sleep with people too quickly. Becoming sexually intimate with someone on or before the third date is too soon for a healthy and balanced relationship to develop. I advise letting the relationship develop for three to six months before bringing sex into it.

POSITIVES TO BE REWARDED FOR

- Getting to the end of this three-part test and being committed to continue reading and working in order to find love. Good for you!
- Being honest with yourself and answering these questions as truthfully as possible.
- Taking responsibility for some (or most) of the reasons you're having trouble in your romantic life.

3

Understanding Your Relationship History

How to Get It Down, Make Sense of It, and Get Over It

In the last chapter, we spent a lot of time focusing on figuring out various aspects of your personality: who you are, what you're like, what you're not like, what you're looking for, and what you're not looking for.

We also spent time looking at your style of dating: the characteristics, values, and personality traits that are most important to you and the ones that aren't so important.

We did all that because it's necessary to know who you are and where you are in terms of dating, life experiences, values, and core issues before you can move forward. When you get a clearer sense of who you are and have a true picture of your starting point, it'll be a lot easier to know which things about yourself and those you date are issues you need to work on.

For this part of the process we came up with a Relationship History Worksheet, and it's a tool that's going to help you see, even more, the patterns in your past so that you can have more control of your relationships in the future.

The reason we came up with this exercise is to translate what I do with clients into something you can do at home to achieve the same objective: to get at your core so that you can get over yourself and find love.

Why is it necessary to write down your history?

Let's say you're reading this book right now because you feel you always date people who end up cheating on you. In order to really examine that we're going to take a very close look at your dating history because, more often than not, between that parade of cheaters I'll bet there were a couple of good people you dated—or could have dated—once or twice. It's important to see that if that's the case—if there were some good ones you rejected because you were more attracted to bad-boy or bad-girl types—then you have to understand why you've been rejecting those good ones.

And to understand why you blame others when at the end of the day, you have had something to do with the state of your love life.

Getting over yourself is a process of taking responsibility for your choices and deciding on the changes you want to make in order to make different—and better—choices in the future.

Fill out the Relationship History Worksheet as thoroughly as possible; it will really help clarify what your past relationships mean in terms of your future chances for love.

CREATE A RELATIONSHIP RECORD

Many people have created family trees for themselves because they want to see—literally, visually—where they come from. Seeing your life mapped out on paper that way can give you a new and powerful perspective on your family's past and history.

In the same way, we're going to create a Relationship Record so that you can see—literally, visually—the history of your love life, your dating life, and all your past relationships.

When we're done, you're going to have a document—a record, a log—that contains a synopsis of who you are, what relationship experience you've had, what your dating and relationship strengths are, and what you're hoping to find in your next relationship. By clarifying the pieces of your past, we'll be able to put them together to look at your present and figure out a route to your future.

Part I: Your Goal/Objective

To start, we're going to come up with a short description of what you hope to accomplish by creating this Relationship Record—why and to what end, basically, you're trying to get over yourself.

Most people have trouble putting things into words—and especially putting things into as few words as possible—so I'm going to give you a bunch of choices: common and general goals and objectives that most people who come to see me have. My clients may not articulate these goals in so many words, but at the end of the interview I usually have a pretty good sense of why they've come to see me even if they don't.

Obviously, most people who come to see me—and most of you reading this book—have one basic goal:

To find love.

And while this is the core of your goal it's helpful to be a little more specific and to take into account what stage of the process you're at. Here are some more specific reasons that people come to see me and why you might be reading this book:

- To find love. Period.
- To start dating
- To get out more
- To get back out there after a divorce or breakup
- To have fun with someone new
- To make friends and widen my social network
- To improve my dating skills or acquire some I don't have

Part II: Relationship History and Experience

The second part of this Relationship Record is the main part of the worksheet—the part where you will list your past relationships and describe them in as much detail as possible. Remember: This is a private document. It's just for you to look at so that you can get a sense of your relationship history in a glance, like flipping through a scrapbook or a photo album. This part of the exercise will provide you with a snapshot of your past—one that you can look at and study to find clues about what has caused you trouble in your previous relationships.

If you have the time and the energy, start as far back as possible—college, high school, junior high school, even elementary school—because I guarantee you that you'll see a pattern emerge from the list as soon as it starts taking shape.

Were all your past boyfriends or girlfriends athletes or cheerleaders?

Were they all brainiacs?

Were they all blond?

Were they all troubled?

Were there not any boyfriends or girlfriends?

This is the place to put down as much information as possible—as many names, dates, details, memories, and thoughts as you can remember about all your relationships: short or long, requited or unrequited. Because even your crushes or virtual relationships online can shed important additional light on your relationship history and fill in a lot of the blanks about what types of people and relationships you have a habit of being drawn to. In fact, sometimes those are the most important details you can possibly include.

Just to get you started, I'm going to give you some types of relationships to think about including when you make your list:

- Intense flirtations (live)
- Intense flirtations (online)
- Short-term relationships (less than three months)
- Long-term relationships (exclusive, monogamous, and lasting longer than eight months)
- Nonspecified relationships of medium duration (casual dating, semi-serious dating, anything longer than a one-night stand, vague or difficult to categorize situations)
- Cohabitations
- Engagements (current and/or broken)
- Marriages
- Divorces
- Other

A sample entry in this section could look something like this:

1995–1997: Long-term relationship with Bob Brown.
Met in college but didn't date. Lived together as roommates for six months before becoming romantically involved. Favorite couple activities included: seeing movies, watching the Yankees, Asian-style cooking, sex. Main problems: He was a sports junkie, really messy, and wouldn't commit after two years. Things I wish Bob had done differently: paid as much attention to me as he did to the World Series, the Super Bowl, the Final Four, and Wimbledon; picked up his socks more often (or at all); asked me to marry him. Things I wish I had done differently: expressed my need for attention more; not nagged as much about the messiness of the apartment; not confused great sex with a promising long-term commitment-bound relationship—which, in the end, it wasn't. It sucked.

Or this:

1967: Crush (unrequited) on Suzie Smith
Shared a desk with her in Mrs. O'Malley's first grade classroom. Attracted to Suzie's blond pigtails, cute plaid dresses, and the way she always seemed to have all the answers. Can trace my love of smart blondes all the way back to Suzie. Tried to play with her at recess but she was too busy with that kid Christopher whose last name I can't remember because he was so good at kickball, prison ball, and the hundred-yard dash. Felt the sting of unreturned love fully; got over it by second grade when I laid eyes on Wendy White.

Or this:

2002 (January to June): Obsessed with Matt Damon
2002 (July to December): Dated Mike Denon,
 who looked just like Matt Damon
Which is about all I can remember about him. Except for the fact that he was my first celebrity-inspired boyfriend. And, thankfully, my last.

For extra credit, try putting photos to these entries. Go through your desk drawers, computer files, and photo albums and find pictures of your old boyfriends or girlfriends and clip them to your Relationship History Worksheet. This will provide a very useful visual aid to help you:

- Remember who they were.
- Remember what they looked like and why you were attracted to them.
- Remember what was good about the relationship.
- Remember what was bad about the relationship.
- Determine whether or not you were truly happy when you were together by looking at your appearance and demeanor if you're in the photo.

Part III: Dating Skills and Assets

When you're finished, this part of the exercise will show you at a glance all the things you're especially good at and what positive assets you have that make you a good date and will likely make you successful at finding love when you start your search.

Remember, though: This list of skills and assets shouldn't be padded or exaggerated as if you're trying to sell yourself. The objective here is to be as honest with yourself as possible. Instead of exaggerating or inventing good points and strengths, focus on the fact that we're listing your positive qualities here, not your negative ones.

To help you along, here are some sample skills and assets you might have that would be good to add to your list:

- Terrific sense of humor
- Big brown eyes
- Great attitude
- Full head of hair
- Good with kids, parents, and pets
- Nice to waiters/big tipper
- Excellent manners
- Not afraid to say I'm sorry or admit I'm wrong
- Can appreciate a good dirty joke
- Cry at movies/in touch with my feminine side

- Love the blues
- Don't smoke
- Am not a vegan
- Vote in every election
- Can change a flat
- Can make a perfect omelet
- Can make conversation with almost anyone
- Health-conscious but will still eat carbs

What follows is the Relationship History Worksheet in its entirety, which, when completed, will be your Relationship Record. Feel free to make additional copies of the Relationship Experience pages of the template so you can create a truly detailed chronicle of all your past relationships.

RELATIONSHIP HISTORY WORKSHEET

Complete this worksheet and you'll have a much clearer picture of your personal relationship history. This detailed list of who you've been involved with, how long it lasted, and why it ended will provide you with extremely useful information and clues to who you are and what issues you need to focus on in the future to improve your success in dating.

YOUR NAME

CITY/STATE

AGE

OCCUPATION

KIDS

PETS

HOBBIES/PASSIONS

I. GOAL(S)

Write down any and all goals you hope to achieve through the process of getting over yourself. These goals can include all areas and aspects of your life in addition to dating and relationships.

II. RELATIONSHIP EXPERIENCE

Here is where you can record details about your past relationships. You can focus on only your significant relationships or you can broaden the worksheet to include blind dates, crushes, platonic friendships, online connections, short-term relationships, and any other emotional or physical involvements you've had during the recent past or over the course of your lifetime. Remember that the more details you provide here, the more comprehensive the picture you'll have of your dating and relationship history. You can use the template provided to collect the relevant information about these relationships, or you can make up your own templates.

DATE OF RELATIONSHIP_____

NAME_____

TYPE/LENGTH_____

HOW YOU MET_____

WHAT ATTRACTED YOU_____

WHY YOU BROKE UP_____

WHO ENDED THE RELATIONSHIP_____

PROS_____

CONS_____

PHOTO OF HIM/HER

PHOTO OF THE TWO
OF YOU

DETAILS
_____
_____
_____

BEST MEMORY
_____
_____
_____

WORST MEMORY
_____
_____
_____

BIGGEST ISSUE/PROBLEM/OBSTACLE/CONFLICT
_____
_____
_____

THINGS I WISH I HAD DONE DIFFERENTLY
_____
_____
_____

DATE OF RELATIONSHIP _____

NAME _____

TYPE/LENGTH _____

HOW YOU MET _____

WHAT ATTRACTED YOU _____

WHY YOU BROKE UP _____

WHO ENDED THE RELATIONSHIP _____

PROS _____

CONS _____

PHOTO OF HIM/HER

**PHOTO OF THE TWO
OF YOU**

DETAILS

_____
_____
_____

BEST MEMORY

_____
_____
_____

WORST MEMORY

_____
_____
_____

BIGGEST ISSUE/PROBLEM/OBSTACLE/CONFLICT

_____

_____

_____

THINGS I WISH I HAD DONE DIFFERENTLY

_____

_____

_____

Here is where you can think about and record your thoughts about the relationships you just described. Think about any commonalities and patterns you see in any aspects of those relationships. Use this template to help you see these issues.

Patterns/Similarities in Appearance of the People You've Dated
(e.g., blond, brunette, tall, short, extremely attractive)

_____

_____

_____

Patterns/Similarities in Personality of the People You've Dated
(e.g., introverted, extroverted, controlling, passive, kind, compassionate, passionate, edgy, ambitious, type A, laid-back)

_____

_____

_____

Patterns/Similarities in What Attracted You to the People You've Dated
(e.g., great personality, hot body, big job, financial status, chemistry, intellectual connection, cultural/religious similarities, common hobbies/ passions, attractive lifestyle)

_____

_____

_____

**Patterns/Similarities in Problems/Issues
You've Had in These Relationships**
(e.g., fidelity/cheating, boredom, problems with exes, commitment issues,
difference in sex drives, neediness issues, etc.)

_____

_____

_____

**In Your Most Serious Committed Relationships,
What Are the Three Things You Would Have Done Differently?**
In Other Words: What Things Do You Think You Did Wrong and
How Would You Change Them?

_____

_____

_____

Other Thoughts

_____

_____

_____

III. YOUR SKILLS AND ASSETS

This is where I want you to list your skills and assets—all the positive qualities and attributes that make you attractive and dateable to potentials.
Don't be shy and don't be afraid to brag. This is where you want to think
about your best traits and selling points.

LOOKS/APPEARANCE

_____

_____

_____

PERSONALITY

_____

_____

_____

CAREER/ARTISTIC ACCOMPLISHMENTS

_____

_____

_____

PEOPLE/RELATIONSHIP SKILLS

_____

_____

_____

BELIEFS/VALUES

_____

_____

_____

LIFE EXPERIENCES/OBSTACLES OVERCOME

_____

_____

_____

OTHER

_____

_____

_____

4

Self-Diagnosis

Identifying the True Problem Behind Your Behavior so You Can Stop It, Fix It, and Get Over It

Chances are, if you're having trouble dating, you—and you alone—have something to do with it. People often think the problem is external—"My dates have all been jerks" is a common reason I hear for why things never work out—but I can tell you from years of experience that while external factors play a part, most of the time, most people's problems with dating and finding love are their own.

Like agreeing to date jerks!

If you can't make it to a good matchmaker or a good life coach or a good therapist, anything that gets you to look at yourself and your behavior—and gets you in the habit of being more self-aware and self-reflective—can be tremendously helpful when embarking on the search for love. Which is why identifying yourself and the types of people you commonly date is so important.

There's an appendix at the back of the book called "A Field Guide to Dating Types," which you can refer to as you read on. Spend some time there to find out what type of dater you are and what type of dater has been *your* type.

Identifying your problem behaviors in dating—figuring out if it's your tough-girl attitude that's turning men off, or your controlling behavior that's turning women off, to name only two annoying and problematic behaviors—is a very important step.

DATING TROUBLE ISN'T THE PROBLEM—
IT'S A SYMPTOM OF *OTHER* PROBLEMS

This is crucial to understand: If you're having trouble finding love, chances are dating is not your main problem. Chances are your trouble with dating is a **symptom** of other problems—larger, deeper emotional issues that are at the core of who you are.

Those larger and deeper emotional issues—your core—will be covered in depth in the next section of the book, but first you need to identify them. Taking a cold, hard look at yourself and developing a deeper understanding of who you are and why is one of the most important and fundamental parts of the process of finding love. Many of the people who come to me show up because they've spent much of their life avoiding themselves and not looking at what their own issues are and why they have them. They've spent years having trouble in relationships or not having any relationships because they've been too afraid to sit themselves down and try to get to the true cause of their dating difficulties.

The problem with avoiding your core is that it eventually catches up with you. You can run but you can't hide from the fiber of your being—your childhood, your hurts, your wounds, the relationships that have formed you and made you who you are today, good or bad. Almost everyone tries to outrun their past, but eventually you will arrive at a point at which you know there's nowhere left to go but inside.

Some problems are easier to solve than others. Some clients come to me with issues that are relatively easy to fix once those issues are identified.

Maybe it's a question of low self-esteem for someone who has gained weight after a bad breakup or after a long period of being alone. Starting a fitness program or weight loss program might be just the spark they need to get them back on track and feeling better about themselves. Maybe it's a question of making some adjustments in clothes and makeup to stop sending the wrong message. Choosing clothes that aren't as provocative and revealing and toning down the mannequin-like makeup can help someone stop attracting the wrong kind of guy. I'm not saying don't be sexy—I'm just saying less is more.

Some other issues—usually of trust or social awkwardness or deep emotional scarring—require more help than a matchmaker can give, which is why I'll often suggest to someone whose problems are of a sensitive nature or seem very deep-seated that they seek professional counseling from a trained therapist who can help them on a level that I can't.

But for most of the people I see and for most of you reading this book, a few basic, fundamental—and relatively easy to fix— problems are the most common causes of dating difficulties.

PROBLEM BEHAVIORS IN DATING = SELF-PROTECTIVE BEHAVIORS

Once you've identified your problem behavior(s), you need to connect the dots to what's behind them and to understand what emotional wounds or painful life experiences have caused you to develop these behaviors. Connecting those dots won't solve your problems instantly. It might take awhile to change your behavior and make peace with some of your issues, but it's still a crucial step in understanding that your behavior and emotional health are contributing factors in your relationship history.

Probably the biggest revelation to most of my clients is when, after our long first interview and after I've figured out what makes them tick and why, I explain to them that their problematic dating behaviors are self-protective: that is, they've developed ways to protect themselves from being vulnerable to anything from emotional injury to plain old disappointment. Once my clients understand that connection—that their appearance-related problems, for example, are related to the fact that they're afraid of getting hurt again or that their overly promiscuous behavior is a way to avoid true and meaningful connection because they have trust issues—they begin to see much more clearly who they are and how they come across to other people. And it's at this point that they begin to realize that the more they understand themselves—the more they know who they really are, instead of who they just think they are—the better chance they'll have in their search for love.

OUTWARD BEHAVIORS—A.K.A. "GARAGE DOORS"— AND WHAT'S BEHIND THEM

I call these problematic self-protective behaviors "garage doors" because they keep you inside yourself and away from what you really want to find: love. Garage door behaviors are what we hide behind when we're not ready to get out there and date, and they're what must be lifted and opened if you're ever going to get over yourself and find love.

I'm going to help you diagnose yourself by showing you some of the most common dating problems and how these problems can affect your success in dating and ultimately in finding love. In each case, I'll show you the outward behavior and then the underlying cause. As you read, think about what garage door behaviors you have and why, and what they've been protecting you from doing or feeling.

Case Study 1
Outward Behavior: Extreme Pickiness
Underlying Cause: Fear of Being Hurt—Again

Dating is a process of selection, from scanning a room full of potentials in a crowded bar to deciding in the first few minutes of a first date whether the person sitting across from you is your type. Being selective in your choices is a necessary and healthy part of finding love. Being careful in your screening process can weed out certain types who might not be good for you, people who are dishonest or self-centered or who send up other red flags when you meet them and start to get to know them. Having a certain level of choosiness can protect you from getting involved in bad relationships. At the very least, having some set standards can help you narrow down your choices and increase your chances of succeeding at dating by understanding what traits—tangible and intangible—are important to you and which ones you're willing to compromise on.

But normal selectivity—or pickiness—isn't what we're talking about here. In the case of the Extremely Picky Dater, we're talking about an almost pathological level of sensitivity: people who have a laundry list of requirements that someone has to have in order to be even considered as a potential date.

I've had clients who are kind of picky. They claim to prefer guys who are a certain height, or women who have a certain color eyes and like a certain kind of music or sport or cuisine. Within reason, these short lists of preferences help us narrow down our search for love and help us find a person who will be good company, someone we can go out and do things with, and who might become something more. And then I've had clients who are *extremely picky*. These clients walk in with a long list of requirements that go far beyond the normal and acceptable list of preferences we all have.

Most of the Extremely Picky Daters I've encountered are women, and they're really something. They have long lists of required qualities, physical attributes, financial offerings, and sexual performance levels that they measure potential partners against.

Big house?

Check.

Fancy car?

Check.

Great legs, firm butt, and a full head of hair?

Check. Check. Check.

Willing to take Viagra?

Get over yourself!

Not only are these Extremely Picky Daters obnoxious, but they're also annoying, since most of the time they're looking for things they don't offer themselves. Like a high-paying job or a great pension plan when they don't even have a job. Or a hot bod when they could stand to lose a few.

Plenty of men are extremely picky, too—they want to meet twenty-year-old women when they're pushing fifty, and they want those twenty-year-olds to have long blond hair when they themselves are bald.

These men clearly need to get over themselves, too.

Most of the time when I've dealt with clients like this, their lists haven't helped them find love. In fact, their lists have usually hurt them.

The first step in helping an Extremely Picky Dater is to make them understand that if they're ever going to get over themselves and find love, they're going to have to get rid of the list: throw it in a lake or destroy it in some sort of ceremonial way to mark the fact that they're starting a whole new chapter of their dating life—a successful one because they are more flexible and accepting and less rigid and demanding.

Getting rid of the actual list is one thing, but getting rid of it in their head means figuring out why they're so picky in the first place—why they're ruling out almost every single person on the planet because these people don't measure up and why they're making it virtually impossible for themselves to find love.

Lots of picky daters have lots of issues. They've either been deeply disappointed in past relationships—getting involved with people who haven't treated them special enough—or they're still getting over the old wounds of a divorce or breakup. Both factors were the case with Cynthia, a client of mine in her late forties. Long divorced and having recently ended a two-year relationship with a guy because he "just wasn't that into her," Cynthia came to me with a four-page single-spaced typed list that she carried in her wallet like a form of identification—which it actually was, since anyone she tried to date ended up figuring out that she was the Picky One, with her *Must be over 6'0" but under 6'4"/Must love dogs and hate cats/Must eat only organic food* demands. Cynthia was wary of getting involved again and had convinced herself that making a list of requirements for a future relationship would help her be more careful and make better choices when it came to dating.

Other picky daters are like another client, Elyse, who was pushing fifty and had never been married. Elyse didn't have an actual written list when she came to see me, but she was so dismissive of potentials as being deficient in almost every way that she hadn't had a real date—much less a real relationship—in more than a decade. The more we talked, the more I realized that the root of her pickiness was a troubled relationship with her father, who had always been extremely critical of her looks and almost always forgot her birthday.

Elyse' extreme level of pickiness had become a big thick garage door that served as a protective shield: Reject others before they can reject you. Who in their right mind would want to get involved with a woman who had such a long list of demands?

You may not have an actual list written out or typed and single-spaced, but if you're an Extremely Picky Dater you probably have that list in your head—a long list of unrealistic and ridiculous and impossible expectations—a list that you've unconsciously made in order to protect yourself from getting involved in relationships. No one could ever measure up to all the requirements and no one would want to even if they could. And you've probably done that to protect yourself because you were hurt and don't want to be hurt again.

Get Over Yourself Solution: Lose the list, whether it's on paper or in your head; deal with your issues; and get over yourself so that you can finally find the love you want.

Case Study 2
Outward Behavior: Can't Flirt
Underlying Cause: Insecurity and Low Self-Esteem

Everybody knows a woman who can't flirt. The one who's either talking sports with the bartender or doing something annoying to the guy on the next bar stool, like picking a fight about politics or the latest reality show.

She's the one who's always a *girl friend,* never the *girlfriend.*

I haven't just known this type. I *was* this type—the perpetual buddy—and that's how I became a matchmaker: by fixing up my friends and giving them advice because I myself wasn't dating. Which is why I have real empathy for my clients, especially for this particular type of dater.

I'm always amazed when clients who can't flirt have jobs that require them to be upbeat and positive—jobs in public relations or party planning or sales. They're paid to be a people person at the office and are bubbly and vivacious on the job, but they're the complete opposite in their personal lives. I've seen lots of women who can't flirt and who are clueless when it comes to guys even though they're in the game—going out with friends and hitting the bar scene and outwardly open to meeting guys. The problem is that they're playing all wrong.

Women who can't flirt have a few behaviors in common: they usually have a defensive attitude, an aggressive and sometimes even openly hostile manner, and a lack of softness. Just like Stephanie, a cute but too-tough twentysomething who was like a pit bull in pumps: ripping into any guy who made the mistake of trying to engage her in conversation when she was sitting at a bar with a sarcastically nasty comment, even though that's why she was there—to meet and talk to guys!

Or like Beth, an attractive brunette with a great smile who just would not shut up about all the things she didn't like about herself.

These flirtationally challenged women are like girls in elementary school who pull boys' hair to get attention—just as annoying and just as immature.

Despite the fact that most of the time these women are cute and smart, they're usually instant turnoffs to guys because none of their good qualities come out when they go out. There's no eye contact, no hair-flipping, no occasional and gentle physical contact—none of the subtle things women do to be engaging or attractive to men with the purpose of drawing them into a conversation and possibly something more.

Women who can't flirt display none of the charm or sweetness—or sexiness—of a woman trying to connect with a man. Just a lot of sarcasm and hard edges.

Sometimes the roots for this inability to flirt go deep. I've learned that some women are this way because they were never popular with boys unless they wanted to watch sports together or talk about the boys' girlfriend problems. Being the kind of girl guys instantly see as "just a friend" instead of a possible romantic girlfriend does a number on a woman's self-confidence, so it's no wonder that women like this—perpetual buddies—often feel scarred. They're so used to feeling unattractive and unfeminine and essentially invisible to the men they meet that they don't have any dating skills.

Women who can't flirt become so convinced over time that the men they meet are only interested in friendship that they don't know how to act when they approach men—or how to react when men approach them.

Often women who can't flirt need a little coaching—flirting lessons, if you will—to get them going and give them some of the fundamental dating skills they lack. Like being nice.

But just as important as mastering basic dating skills (or at least practicing them a few times) is getting this type of woman to face her lifelong insecurity and cripplingly low self-esteem—issues that have plagued her most of her life and have affected her ability to date. Because lots of times, when a woman isn't nice to the men she's trying to attract, she often isn't nice to herself, which means that one of the least attractive aspects of this type of dater is that they engage in a lot of self-deprecating humor. It's one thing to have a sense of humor about yourself, but when the butt of your jokes is always you and you constantly talk about yourself in the least flattering terms, men aren't going to find you very appealing or attractive.

Which shouldn't be that surprising.

How can you expect someone to like you when you don't like yourself?

Women who can't flirt often have to be scared straight: they have to understand that if they don't learn how to communicate properly with the opposite sex and how to stop picking on themselves, it's going to take them a long, long time to find love.

Get Over Yourself Solution: If you're one of those women who can't flirt and is turning off the men you're supposed to be turning on, stop criticizing and insulting yourself, and start being nice—to you and to the men you're out with. This means working on your self-esteem so that the men you meet can see that you're adorable and smart and a real catch.

Case Study 3
Outward Behavior: Too Busy to Date
Underlying Causes: Procrastination and Avoidance

I've had lots of clients I've called Mr. Busy. Mr. Busy types remind me of my brother, who we used to call Five-Job Jimmy because, well, he had a lot of jobs. These are usually great guys—warm, honest, and fun to be around.

That is, if you can find them.

Like my brother, Jimmy, did when we were growing up, Mr. Busy types either have one really demanding job, or two or three jobs they juggle. They're overextended in every possible way—coaching their kid's soccer and baseball teams, volunteering at the local soup kitchen or fund-raising for their favorite charity, very involved with a hobby that takes up enough time to be another full-time job. On the rare occasions that Mr. Busy is home, he's swamped with home improvement projects that he insists are going to help him attract and keep the woman of his dreams.

You know, the woman he hasn't met yet because he hasn't had time to go on any dates.

Mr. Busy types think that finding love is the next piece in their life puzzle.

To me, it's the *only* piece of their puzzle.

But if they want love, they're first going to have to devote some time to finding it.

Finding love isn't what you do in your spare time: it's what you commit yourself to doing all the time. If you're here reading this book, chances are you finally see that you have to get over yourself and some of your issues in order to find love, and making time to go on dates and meet people is the first, most basic part of the process.

Simple as it sounds, making time to find love requires that you make your search a priority, and making it a priority means you're ready, willing, and able to connect with people. And just as with other types of daters, Mr. Busy types often aren't quite there yet.

Being too busy to date is another garage door behavior because packing your schedule with too many activities and obligations and plans prevents you from having a relationship. A man who doesn't have time to date is almost always a man who is afraid to date—afraid to risk getting close to someone, afraid to risk making himself vulnerable.

If we keep connecting the dots we'll soon find that behind that busy schedule is a guy who was hurt in some way, either in a past relationship or by a traumatic loss that has made him afraid of losing someone or something he doesn't even have. The reason he's putting love last isn't because he's a jerk, but it's probably why he's had trouble with dating and relationships in the past: nothing makes a woman feel less important than a guy who makes her his last priority.

Get Over Yourself Solution: Whether you're a workaholic or an overextended volunteer, examine the reasons why you're avoiding yourself and spending so much time on everything but your search for love. Then, re-prioritize your schedule so that you'll have time to get over yourself and get back in the dating game.

Case Study 4
Outward Behavior: Too Chunky/Dumpy/Frumpy/Lumpy
Underlying Causes: Insecurity, Low Self-Esteem and Confidence,
Fear of Rejection

I've had plenty of clients who were a hundred pounds overweight, but I've had many, many more who were only twenty or thirty or fifty pounds overweight or who haven't changed their hairstyle since the eighties or updated their wardrobe since the nineties. These Chunky/Dumpy/Frumpy/Lumpy types are having trouble with their appearance, and it's causing them to have trouble with dating.

Most of the time, these problems are easy to fix. New clothes, a trip to the salon, joining a gym and committing to a healthier lifestyle are sometimes all it takes to get someone off the couch and into the dating world.

And almost always problems with appearance have a lot, if not everything, to do with self-esteem—a significant breakup or rejection or some other kind of major incident that has shaken their self-confidence enough to make them want to hide.

More often than not it's that impulse to hide that is at the root of weight and appearance issues. Crazy hair, sloppy or eccentric or outdated clothes, and too much weight are the perfect covers under which to hide. It's the perfect protection from having to get back out there and risk more rejection and pain. It's also the perfect way to keep you isolated, keep your wounds from healing, and keep you from finding love again.

Get Over Yourself Solution: Deal with your wounds—rejection or anger or sadness or loneliness. Make a few long-overdue improvements to your appearance and commit to changing some of your unhealthy health habits so that you can feel better about yourself and stop hiding from the love you deserve.

Case Study 5
Outward Behavior: Too Old to Be Acting That Young
Underlying Causes: Low Self-Esteem, Issues with Aging,
Post-Divorce Adjustment

Whether it's the divorced mom with kids who won't leave the bar before closing time or the soon-to-be-middle-aged Party Boy who behaves like an obnoxious frat boy, older singles who can't, don't, or won't act their age have problems.

Most of the people who fall into this category are second-time-arounders—women and men who are divorced and reentering the dating world after long marriages. Often they're unsure how to behave now that they're single again—either they're enjoying their freedom a little too much by overindulging in the dating scene, or their newly gained independence is making them anxious because they're used to being coupled and scared that they're never going to meet anyone again. Whether it's excitement that's motivating them or a fear of loneliness, this type of dater is out partying too much and probably having way too many booty calls for their own good, let alone to be a successful dater.

Other people who fall into this category are more commitment-phobic and narcissistic than sad and lonely because of a change in relationship status. The Party Boy or Player is usually motivated by not wanting to grow up and because of that he wants to keep dating younger and younger girls to feel young and free for as long as possible. But dating twenty-year-olds when you're pushing forty isn't attractive—in fact, it's a red flag for smart, interesting women who are looking for a real connection, not just a night doing shots.

Get Over Yourself Solution: Cut back on the drinking and partying, stop the booty calls, get an age-appropriate attitude, and start acting like who you are instead of who you were twenty years ago so that you can find love.

Case Study 6
Outward Behavior: Too Promiscuous
Underlying Causes: Low Self-Esteem, Still Getting Over an Ex,
Anger Issues

Similar to the Age Inappropriate Dater, the dater who is too easy and overly promiscuous is having trouble in the booty-call department. The person having too much casual sex and behaving in ways that are unsafe physically and emotionally is in just as much trouble as the person who can't get any dates—if not more. Singles who date too much and sleep around too much are problematic: Their lack of selectivity and their need for constant attention is an obvious sign that something isn't right.

Men have been having casual one-night-stand sex for as long as humans have been walking the earth, but most women haven't. Casual sex and one night stands are relatively new for women, byproducts of the sexual revolution and one of the things the modern woman has become all too familiar with. Lots of women think of booty calls as a sign of the success of feminism. It's the idea that women, like men, now have the sexual freedom to go out there and hook up with someone they just met and barely know—but I couldn't disagree more. Promiscuity—whether in the form of club- and bar-hopping one night stands or texting old flames for a late-night house call—is a sign of an unhealthy ego or unresolved emotional issues in both men and women.

Promiscuous behavior is also a garage door behavior, though it's a less obvious one. Many of my clients who sleep around too much say they do it because they're alone and lonely.

I tell them they have it backwards.

I tell them they're alone and lonely *because* they do it.

Hooking up indiscriminately and way too often is what people who are afraid of intimacy do: they guarantee their own failure at dating by sleeping with anyone they can get their hands on.

Sometimes promiscuous behavior is fueled by alcohol. Almost always it's caused by low self-esteem. Whatever's at the root of that dangerously low self-esteem—sadness over the end of a relationship or anger at someone who dumped and rejected you, which is now anger turned inward because instead of respecting yourself you're disrespecting yourself—has to be addressed before you can move on and find real love.

Get Over Yourself Solution: Watch the alcohol, stop the booty calls, and figure out what's making you treat yourself with so much disregard and disrespect so that you can be ready for true love when it comes back around.

Case Study 7
Outward Behavior: Too Shy, Awkward, and Inexperienced
Underlying Causes: Low Self-Esteem, Sexual Confusion, Trust Issues

I've seen thousands of clients who are shy, awkward, and therefore inexperienced at dating. The Shy Awkward Dater has so much trouble meeting people and carrying on a conversation that they often can't even get to the starting line—the first date—much less the finish line of a second or third date.

Lots of Shy Awkward Daters are shy and awkward because they're out of practice. For whatever reason, they've been out of the dating game for so long that their basic social skills are rusty. For this type, a little bit of coaching from me as to what to talk about and what not to talk about, how to make eye contact and how to flirt, how to feel more comfortable in their own skin and get out of their own way is all they need to get them on their way to finding love. You'll find more about this in greater detail in the second half of the book.

Daters who are *extremely* shy and awkward, though, are different. They're among the toughest type of client to help because all too often their shyness and awkwardness are rooted in some very deep emotional issues. Sometimes they've been the victims of abuse or have other issues relating to trust and intimacy that are more serious than those of the average dater. In cases like this I almost always recommend that they seek counseling or therapy first to help them get a firm grasp on their past before they turn their full attention to dating. They'll have a much better chance of becoming a successful dater and ultimately finding love in the future if they have some professional help dealing with their past.

Get Over Yourself Solution: Get coached or get help before going out and looking for love.

Case Study 8
Outward Behavior: Narcissistic
Underlying Causes: Narcissism, Low Self-Esteem

I make no secret that narcissists are my least favorite type of dater to deal with, both because their egotistic and self-centered behavior is annoying and because they're often completely resistant to change.

Daters who display more than just a few narcissistic traits and who could probably even be diagnosed as having pathological narcissism or Narcissistic Personality Disorder (NPD)—"Ns," as I call them—are rampant out there in the dating world, and they're truly daters to avoid at all costs. Daters with NPD are very destructive since they seduce and abandon the people they get involved with and inflict a great deal of emotional pain, suffering, and injury on them.

But more common than the pathological narcissist is the garden-variety type: the Narcissistic Dater. People who are narcissistic (as opposed to actual narcissists) do things we commonly think of as self-absorbed: talk about themselves too much, brag about their accomplishments and possessions, show no interest in the other person and ask them no questions. The narcissistic guy is the guy so full of himself he can't stop looking at his reflection in the mirror at the bar or can't stop telling you how many cars he owns or how much money he has, and he's the kind of dater who has developed behaviors like bragging and showing off to overcompensate for the fact that he feels like a nobody.

Again, we're back to the all too common cause of almost all of these garage door behaviors: low self-esteem. And, again, we're seeing how low self-esteem can adversely affect your dating life. Narcissistic men and women behave like you're lucky to meet them, lucky to be out with them, and lucky to sleep with them even though, deep down, they feel unworthy and fear rejection, and even though their inflated sense of self and nonstop self-absorption is often a huge turnoff.

If I'm lucky—and if they're lucky—they'll get it once I point it out to them and realize that unless they stop talking about them-selves and start showing some interest in and listening to the person sitting across the table, they're going to be alone for a very long time.

Get Over Yourself Solution: Recognize that you're a little too into yourself and make a conscious effort to focus on and talk about someone else—such as your date. Ask them questions, and listen to understand, not to respond. Then responding becomes natural. You'll see how connecting with another person can improve your self-esteem and help you find love.

Part Two

getting to your core

5

Facing Your Demons

Going Back to Where You Don't Want to Go so You Can Finally Move On

In the first section of this book, I talked about what usually happens when I meet a new client:

- I have them fill out some general questionnaires about their likes and dislikes, interests and hobbies, and past relationships.
- I ask them a ton of questions during an almost ninety-minute interview.
- I take a short break to decide if I'm going to work with them or not.

Often, that last item—deciding on whether I'm going to work with a client—is the hardest part of the interview. Because it's at that point that I have to process everything I've heard—all their issues, their difficulties, their painful experiences, their hopes and expectations—and figure out if I think I can help them.

Sometimes, to be honest, one of the factors in my decision-making process is a client's basic likability. It might sound unfair of

A PERSONAL NOTE: MY OWN DEMONS

This particular area—the area of facing your demons—is one I know a lot about, because when I finally faced my own demons more than five years ago the healing that took place in my life and in my spirit and in my core was truly life changing.

It was one of the hardest and lowest points of my life, a period of a few years during which my marriage ended and my father died. When I got through it—when I grieved for the losses I'd had and faced the mistakes I'd made and the negative ways I'd always dealt with painful times in my life, and after I'd made some long overdue and very important changes—I knew I was now completely true to myself and true to my core in a way I'd never been before.

I'd faced my demons, finally.

I'd figured out the things I could have done differently and forgiven myself for my mistakes.

I'd forgiven the people who had hurt me.

And I got over a lot of what was keeping me from finding happiness—true happiness—for most of my life.

And it was a truly spiritual experience.

I won't go into too many more details—this book, after all, is about you—except to say that my own effort to face my demons has given me a real connection to and deep empathy for the love-challenged people I work with.

And for you, reading this book.

For many people, just hearing someone else's story is enough to inspire them to deal with and survive their own problems, because they no longer feel so alone.

And they no longer feel like things will never get better.

Which is one of the messages I'm here to give you: Things can get better.

And they will get better.

Once you articulate the demons, once you let go of the pain and the guilt and the shame and the anger and the sadness they've filled you with, once you see all the ways those demons have affected you and the physical and emotional toll they've taken on you—they will go away.

And in their place—into that clean empty place you will soon have in your heart and in your core—will come the love that you're ready to find. And healthy enough to hold on to.

me to decide against taking on a new client because I don't like them, but at the end of the day, I'm probably much more accepting than most of my clients waiting to be matched. If I think someone is essentially unlikable, then they're going to be very hard to match.

It's one thing to have flaws; that's the essence of being human. Being unlikable—arrogant, smart-alecky, and, for lack of a better way to put it, generally not nice—is another thing completely, and it's an instant indicator that this is a client I'm probably not going to take on.

Most of the time, though, my decisions don't depend on a client's general likability or lack thereof. Most of the time my decisions are based on whether I think a potential client can face their demons—those deepest and most painful issues that have gotten into our cores like evil spirits and end up influencing our behavior in ways that harm us and keep us from finding happiness and love.

Again, being flawed—having problems and behaviors that have gotten in the way of your life in general and your dating life in particular—is not the issue. Not only does every single person in the world have issues of one kind or another, but also it's those very parts of our personalities and our personal histories—our deepest wounds—that make us unique individuals. And it's often those deep wounds that make people worthy of love. The harder they've fought and the farther they've walked to get to this starting place, the more they deserve happiness and the more they treasure it once they find it.

So, assuming a new client gets through the interview, demons and all, and I'm convinced they're ready to face their pasts and get to their cores, all in order to start fresh and find love, I return to my office, sit back down at my desk across from them and tell them that if they're ready to work with me, I'm ready to work with them.

And then we get started.

LEARNING TO LOOK AT YOUR PAST AND LEARN FROM IT

I always tell clients that I can introduce them to the perfect person but if they haven't worked on themselves it won't matter because they won't be ready to connect with someone else.

Which is why my coaching begins in the interview.

But the coaching I'm talking about now has nothing to do with what they look like or what they're wearing or what they need to do less or more of in order to find love.

This part of the coaching is where I get them to confront their past.

And it isn't easy.

Because I have to take them back to that uncomfortable place inside themselves—the place where their deepest sadness and most painful wounds are—and help them look around.

Once we start looking inside that place and looking at where they've been and what they've experienced in their life, I'll start to ask questions.

I'll say, "Tell me the truth about what happened in your last relationship. Not what he or she did wrong but what *you* did wrong."

I'll say, "Tell me why you always pick someone who doesn't treat you well, or who hurts you. Tell me why you don't feel worthy of someone who will treat you with love and respect."

Then I'll get quiet.

I'm waiting for the answer.

I'm waiting for the truth.

And nearly all the time, people tell me the truth, because there's so much good in them.

They tell me the painful parts of their past—relationships, marriages, breakups, divorces, the people and events that have hurt them the most and the things from which they think they'll never recover. And I listen.

What I almost always hear when I'm helping someone face their demons is insecurity and low self-esteem.

And insecurity and low self-esteem is almost always caused by this:

Rejection. And fear of loss.

Rejection by a parent, rejection by a boyfriend or girlfriend, husband or wife—or the loss of a parent early in life—can cause big problems with intimacy.

Rejection, especially by a parent, is extremely damaging, not just at the time of the actual rejection, but in the aftermath of it, years and years, and failed relationship after failed relationship, later. Rejection sends a message to the recipient that they're not worthy of love, and eventually that message is internalized. The rejected person starts believing the message, starts believing that they're not worthy of love, and very quickly damage is done to their core.

Most of us have been rejected at some point in our life by someone we cared about but fewer of us have suffered real rejection or loss, very early on, in the most emotionally impressionable and formative years of our life: in childhood. The people who have felt this kind of rejection from their parents or who as children lost their parents are the toughest cases to work with, because the seeds of self-loathing and worthlessness and fear of loss were planted so early and so deeply. Because of that, the roots of their insecurity run through their core like an intertwining network of blood vessels. Their low self-esteem—or lack of self-esteem—isn't just in one discrete part of themselves. It's everywhere. It's the very fiber of their being and that makes it very difficult to get rid of.

Difficult, but not impossible.

It requires a great deal of energy and patience and self-understanding to see that your insecurity and low self-esteem are symptoms of the larger wound of rejection, and that that wound is what has caused you to feel badly about yourself, probably for as long as you can remember.

That wound is also what's caused you to feel so bad about yourself that you've probably ended up in other similarly rejecting relationships—relationships where you felt unloved and ignored and as if you didn't matter. As unloved and ignored and worthless as you felt from the original rejection.

Or your fear of loss is so strong that you avoid true intimacy altogether and instead get involved with people on a shallower level so there's less to lose.

Because whether we know it or not, mean to or not, want to or not, we repeat the wounds of our past. And those repeated wounds form a pattern.

Wounds like this are what I'm talking about when I talk about demons. Demons, by definition, have "an evil passion or influence" over us and are a "persistently tormenting force" that is "extremely diligent and skillful" at undermining our confidence and robbing us of experiencing joy and happiness because we dislike ourselves so profoundly.

Rejection is a perfect example of a demon in action. And a perfect example of how one single, primary demon left unchecked can adversely affect the course of our emotional and romantic life.

But rejection, like other demons, is a thing you have to get over if you want to find love.

So at that point in the interview, when we've identified a major theme in someone's life, I tell them to stop and think about it.

If there are several demons, I tell them to take each hurtful moment in their past and think about it: think about the ways they were hurt.

And also about what they could have done differently.

Because it's very rare (*never!* lol) that people are perfect.

And I'll ask them questions until I've gotten the answers I need and enough information to help them use where they've been and what they've experienced as a life lesson.

I'll find out what made a woman so independent she's arrogant.

I'll find out what made a guy get married—and divorced—three times.

I'll find out not just whether someone cheated, but why they cheated.

I don't judge. It's not my place and that's not what I'm about or what I'm there to do. I just need to know.

When a client is brave enough to go there with me, to let me take them back to those unpleasant topics that are difficult to talk about and difficult to admit to—when they're finally ready to voice their hurts and take responsibility for their own actions and behaviors and see that they have something to do with where they are now and where they want to be in the future—then I'll say:

"It's over. Get over it. You can't change it. You're here now, and I want to help you. But these red flags are things you're going to take with you to the next relationship unless you fix them."

Almost always people cry.

Their tears come from the soul.

Once they've cried—once they've gone back to the place that I've taken them to, the incident or relationship or memory that is most painful to them—they're in an emotional and spiritual state where they're going to be more open.

Open to healing.

And open to dating.

If a client has very deep emotional scars, usually related to an abusive childhood or relationship, I'm careful not to venture too far into that very sensitive territory because I'm not a therapist, so I'll tell them to get counseling.

Even the clients who don't have past traumas to deal with—I'll tell many of them to get counseling or to see a therapist, too. But I usually tell them that one of the problems with certain kinds of therapists is that they encourage the blame game. While figuring out the root of their problems, it's crucial to have tools for getting past that blaming point: they need to be instructed on how to get over themselves and their pasts in order to move on with their lives.

Getting over yourself is all about taking responsibility for your own actions—and the outcomes of those actions—so that you don't go through life any longer with a sense of helplessness, a sense that you can't do anything to change your life, that you have absolutely no power or control over anything that happens to you.

Lots of things happen all the time that we have no control over—bad things like disease or death or natural disasters or hard times caused by this terrible economy. But the kind of helplessness I'm talking about here is an emotional helplessness: the feeling of being a victim that a person who has never taken responsibility for their choices and their actions has. That helplessness and sense of victimhood in turn leaves them angry at the world because they feel like they have no control over their own destiny: they are simply at the mercy of the people who they blame for having all the control.

The first thing that these Blamers need to understand is that until they do take responsibility for themselves—and until they face their demons, face their mistakes and their flaws and their disappointments and failures, too, and not just those of others—they won't be able to find love.

And it won't be anyone's fault but their own.

THE MOST COMMON DEMON: ANGER

With most of the clients I've worked with, the issues we're talking about and the demons they're facing have to do with past relationships that haven't worked—breakups they weren't prepared for and didn't expect and didn't want and are still devastated about or sad about, or problematic relationships with their parents that they still don't really understand.

And, more often than not, that they're still angry about.

Anger—or, more specifically, unresolved anger—is one of the most common demons that need to be faced before you can move on and find love. It's an offshoot of rejection, remember, which is why it's very powerful and corrosive and resilient.

I've seen literally hundreds of clients who I discover, within minutes of talking to them, are angry—sometimes very angry—about a past relationship they still haven't gotten over.

The breakup of a twenty-year marriage.

The breakup of a six-month fling.

The breakup of their parents' marriage years and years ago when they were still young.

Or the fact that one or both of their parents are more critical and less loving than they wanted them to be.

To those clients—and especially women, I hate to admit, since women have a harder time letting go of things than men do—I say this:

Get over yourself!

If you're angry because of your divorce fifteen years ago, if you're angry because someone dumped you when you thought you were a great girlfriend, if you're angry about someone cheating on you when you felt you'd given the marriage or the relationship all you had, if you're angry because you feel that whatever happened in your last relationship wasn't fair: Guess what?

You're going to have to get over it already.

And in order to get over it you're going to have to be proactive about fixing your anger issues.

Maybe you need to go to therapy.

Maybe you need to meditate, or take yoga, or work out.

Maybe you need to pray.

Whatever your way is—do it.

And do it soon.

It's time to forgive so you can be forgiven.

Love is about being vulnerable, and if you can't be vulnerable or if you choose not to be vulnerable you won't have love and intimacy in your life.

Because until you get past whatever wound you're not over yet you're not going to be ready to meet and connect with someone new—and find love.

THE SECOND MOST COMMON DEMON: SADNESS

The second most common demon I see in clients who come to see me is sadness—sometimes sadness over the death of a loved one, but more commonly, sadness caused by a broken heart.

The pain of a broken heart is often underestimated and not taken as seriously as emotional pain caused by other more "legitimate" losses like having someone close to you die, but the deep sadness that can be produced by having a relationship end without warning or without your wanting it to can be devastating. The loss of the relationship and the person you've been dating and been intimately involved with—the person you've presumably been in love with—is its own kind of death, and people grieve sometimes with the depth and scope and totality of their being.

Losing love in whatever way you lose it can be incredibly painful, and that pain, that loss, that emotional wound needs to be respected if it's ever going to heal.

But the problem is that most people suffering the loss of love don't see that before they can get over their broken heart they have to understand what happened and why. Too often, this is a part of getting over yourself that is overlooked.

How many of us have dismissed the obsessive and repetitive rantings of a friend who recently got dumped and thought *Enough is enough* with crying over the breakup and that it was time they moved on?

How many of us, when nursing our own broken heart, have felt that no one understood our pain and ended up feeling all the more isolated because of that lack of understanding?

The problem with the broken heart is that, like all wounds, it takes time to heal. One of the biggest clichés there is, and one of the truest, too, is the saying that time heals all wounds.

The problem with recovering from a broken heart is that often there doesn't seem to be an end in sight to the healing process. It seems to go on and on and on without any real improvement in your mood and outlook and energy level, and more important, without any substantive understanding and analysis of what really happened and why.

Sometimes, of course, breakups, like other unexplained and unfair occurrences in life, happen unexpectedly and for no apparent reason. Many people, for instance, who become involved with true narcissists often describe this shocking kind of out-of-the-blue dumping, usually at the six-week or three-month mark, points at which intimacy tends to reach new benchmarks. These breakups truly do come without warning, just when the relationship appears to be in full swing and often before any real problems seem to be the cause.

People who suffer this sort of breakup are a lot like hit-and-run victims. They didn't see the end of the relationship coming because they didn't realize that the person they were involved with was incapable of intimacy. And because they didn't truly know the person they'd gotten so intimately involved with so quickly, they not only have to grieve the loss of the perfect relationship they thought they were in, but they also have to grieve the loss of the person they thought existed who actually didn't exist.

This sort of broken heart is very difficult to recover from because it's based on so much misinformation and misleading behavior—hallmarks of having a relationship with a narcissist. It's also the type of relationship least likely to elicit sympathy from other people. Many times, even if people don't know you're involved with a narcissist, they pick up on the fact that there is something unreal about the relationship, something that isn't quite right: either that it's moving too quickly or that the whole thing sounds just a little too good to be true. And that usually means that when their suspicions turn out to be correct—when the whole thing *was* a little too good to be true and in fact wasn't true at all—they often can't help but feel a little smug.

And that I-told-you-so smugness they get when things go bad means that they're not going to be that sympathetic to your loss and to the long and, to them, overly dramatic arc of your grieving process.

That lack of sympathy and empathy from other people when you're grieving the loss of love can affect people in different ways, but one common thing I've seen it do to the people I've worked with is to make them feel even more alone and isolated. When there's no one to validate your feelings, to treat you with the sort of kindness you need at such a low point in your emotional life, it's natural to feel as if no one understands you. Or even that no one cares. Even if they do care. This usually makes people sink deeper and deeper down into their own sadness and depression and prolongs their recovery even more.

But the main way this lack of sympathy and empathy from others affects the brokenhearted person is that it produces a lack of sympathy and empathy in their core toward themselves. Instead of respecting their hurt and sadness and pain—respecting it enough to treat themselves with kindness and understanding until it passes and until they heal—brokenhearted people often feel angry at themselves for not getting over their broken hearts more quickly.

Self-directed anger often turns into a larger sense of self-loathing for being such a loser, someone who couldn't hold on to the person they thought they loved and who they thought loved them. They feel a building rage because nothing seems fair or ever seems to work out. What began as a deep but contained wound—the wound of one single discrete episode of lost love—has now grown and spread into a much larger wound. It's become the wound of feeling cursed in love or undeserving of love.

And the totality of that hurt in a person only makes it harder for them to heal from the breakup and believe in their ability to be successful at love.

It makes it harder for them to want to get back out there and try again.

It makes it harder for them to believe that they're ever going to find love again.

More than anything, it makes them afraid of getting hurt again in the future because the hurt right now is so unbearable and so devastating and so seemingly endless.

And so the sadness takes over and makes it almost impossible for them to look inward and be introspective and analytical in any productive way—especially in the ways you need to be introspective and analytical after a breakup, no matter how unfair or unexpected that breakup was.

But more often than not, except for the type of breakup described above, breakups don't come out of the blue.

They're not completely unexpected.

They're not something you had absolutely nothing to do with.

Most times, breakups happen for a reason, usually because of basic incompatibility: he liked to go to clubs and you didn't; she had kids to take care of and you didn't; your sex drives were on different settings.

Or because someone cheated.

Or because someone just lost interest.

Most of the time the person who gets dumped has had a hand in why the relationship ended. There are a million reasons why relationships fail and we all contribute to our own failures to connect. Those failures don't make us bad people; they just make us human.

And it's through those failures that we can learn more about ourselves and our behaviors—and our own particular and unique emptiness that we try to fill with people who may not be able to fill that emptiness.

In order to get over a painful breakup, we have to be able to look at our role in it, even if our role was only to be more in love with a person than that person deserved: to have built that person up more than they deserved, or to expect more from that person than they could ever possibly have given us.

We have to look at why a six-week or three-month relationship can devastate you. What is it about you and your emotional makeup that makes you so vulnerable to such complete and utter heartbreak and spiritual collapse after a relatively short time.

These are questions you have to ask yourself. Because the answers to these questions are clues to who you are, and to what happened in that relationship, and to why it happened and what your role was in it.

And until you ask yourself these important questions—until you really think about the answers—you're not going to heal the deep wounds produced by a painful breakup.

And without the self-knowledge and self-awareness and self-love that come from healing, you're not going to be able to move forward and find love again.

THE THIRD MOST COMMON DEMON: CHILDHOOD TRAUMA/ABUSE

Sadly, demons caused by childhood trauma or abuse are something I hear about all too often when my clients tell me their stories. Sometimes it's actual sexual abuse, sometimes it's physical or verbal abuse or abuse witnessed in the home while growing up due to an alcoholic parent, sometimes it's the emotional absence of an alcoholic parent, but whichever variation it is and whatever the specific details are, the demons childhood trauma produces are always the same: fear of intimacy, serious trust issues, and a deep and profound inability to feel a healthy sense of closeness with another person in a love relationship.

I can't tell you how many clients I've worked with who fit this profile. They have wounds and traumas in their pasts so deep and painful and difficult to overcome that I feel a huge sense of empathy for them and a great sense of commitment to help them start the healing process so that they can eventually find the love they so deserve.

One of those clients was Marjorie, who came to me at forty-four because she had never really had an intimate relationship.

Marjorie told me she'd had some tough times in her childhood, but that she'd been able to overcome them in almost every aspect of her life: she'd gotten an MBA and had started a successful business, was active in local and international charity work, and had traveled the world extensively. But there was still one part of her life that hadn't opened up and developed fully in the way that it should have: her love life.

She had everything else going for her. She was attractive, passionate, kind, and intelligent, and she told me that meeting men and having them show interest in her wasn't the problem: the issue was trust. It took her a long time to trust someone and despite the fact that she tried to go very, very slowly with her first boyfriend—who she met when she was forty-three—it just didn't work.

It was clear to me early in my interview with Marjorie that there was an issue of trauma and abuse at the core of her problem with relationships, and when I asked her if someone had hurt her in her past she confirmed my suspicions. She told me that she felt good about her accomplishments and all the ways she'd flourished in her life despite the significant wounds in her past, but she still wanted one more thing:

To find love.

I'd be lying if I said that facing this particular demon is an easy process, or a quick process, or even one that I take on without strongly urging a client to seek additional help from trained professionals, the way I did with Marjorie.

But I can tell you that even if you're someone who's been the victim of sexual abuse or childhood trauma, you can heal and find love.

And I can tell you that because I'm someone who healed from those deep wounds and found love.

There is hope, there is healing, and there is a whole world of happiness and healthy relationships waiting for you on the other side.

If you face your demons.

If you face your demons with the help of someone trained to help you face them.

And if you treat yourself with kindness and compassion and understanding.

If you do all that, I promise that you, too, will find the love you've spent your whole life waiting for.

FACING YOUR DEMONS WORKSHEET

I've said a few times already that my approach and my methods for helping people get over themselves in order to help them find love are based on some simple commonsense beliefs and principles. One of those commonsense beliefs is that there's real value—and an enormous opportunity for healing—in the idea that articulating something is the first big step you need to take to recover from it.

Just saying it or writing it down—or even merely thinking about it—is a huge first step in moving forward into the light of your future and away from the darkness of your past.

Here's a worksheet you can complete to help you do that.

By writing down your demons, by articulating them and getting them down on paper, you will start to relieve yourself of carrying them around with you, all the time, everywhere you go. Your demons, however minor you might think they are, take up valuable space in your soul and in your mind—and in your heart. Getting rid of them will not only give you a feeling of lightness, but it will help give you renewed hope and energy with which to take on the work in the rest of this book.

Take a few minutes to do this "Facing Your Demons" exercise. When you're finished identifying your demons and thinking about them you should feel a well-earned sense of accomplishment.

Because you're that much closer to resolving your deepest and most important issues and removing your biggest obstacles to finding love.

FACING YOUR DEMONS WORKSHEET

1. What do you think your main demons are—the primary unresolved issues or problems that you believe have been holding you back from finding true happiness?

    _____

    _____

    _____

2. How long have you been struggling with these issues?

    _____

    _____

    _____

3. Have you ever tried to get help with these problems? If so, please list the type(s) of counseling you've sought (psychological/psychiatric, religious/spiritual, support group, meditative, other) and whether it was useful.

    _____

    _____

    _____

    _____

4. What do you think are the main difficulties these issues have caused you? Think especially about coping skills or behaviors you might have adopted in order to manage your pain, sadness, or anger (overeating/weight gain, alcohol/substance abuse, job loss, relationship failures, promiscuity, celibacy, depression, anxiety).

_____

_____

_____

5. Who, besides yourself, do you think is most affected by these issues (e.g., children, siblings, coworkers, potential dates)? How?

_____

_____

_____

6. Who, besides yourself, do you think would benefit most from you successfully facing and dealing with your demons?

_____

_____

_____

7. If you're angry about the failure of a past relationship, please describe what, if anything, you think the other person did to cause the relationship to end.

_____

_____

_____

8. Now describe what, if anything, you think you did to cause the relationship to end.

_____

_____

_____

9. Do you feel ready to face your demons and do the hard work required for getting past them? If yes, explain why. If no, explain why.

_____

_____

_____

10. Think about and write down any friends or family who you think are most understanding of your demons. Think about and write down any friends or family who you think share similar demons.

_____

_____

_____

11. Think about and make some notes about what you could do to help yourself along in the process of facing your demons and getting closer to your goal of finding love.

_____

_____

_____

6

The Mind/Body/Soul Connection

How to Cleanse, Heal, and Improve
Your Three Layers of Being

We spent the last chapter talking all about demons: what they are, how they affect us, and how to face them with the intention and purpose of getting over them and moving toward a better emotional state.

And, of course, toward finding love.

So assuming you've done that or, at least, started to do that—started to identify your demons, think about them, and figure out ways that you're going to proactively work to overcome them—we can head into the next phase of getting over yourself.

THE MIND/BODY/SOUL CLEANSE

You can divide the human self into as many or as few parts as you like, but the way I look at it, there are three parts that need to be specifically addressed in order to properly and completely get rid of old wounds and hurts. These three areas of our being are burdened with sad, heavy thoughts and energy that need to be "cleansed" in order to make room for what will come next: love. These are the mind, the body, and the soul. All three need attention before you can move on.

Facing your demons was the crucial preamble to this step. Without identifying what's been holding you back or affecting you adversely your whole life and then making strides to heal yourself, you won't be ready for the cleansing phase. If you need a little more time with your demons, take it before moving forward. When you enter this phase you need to be truly ready to finish the cleaning-up process you've started.

In short, the point of the mind/body/soul cleanse is to find your inner core and get comfortable with it, because in order to merge worlds with someone else—to connect with your mind and your body and your soul to another human being, which is what finding love is all about—you have to connect with yourself first.

We talked about this in an earlier chapter, too—the necessity of looking at your true self instead of avoiding yourself and inventing a whole other person who doesn't actually exist—and how difficult that sometimes is to do. So many people avoid looking at themselves with a cold hard eye because they don't understand that part of the looking process is a healing process. Seeing yourself for who you truly are and being kind to yourself in ways that you may never have been before, will let you stop the long-ingrained habit of hating yourself. Instead of looking at your faults and your flaws with self-loathing, you'll look at your faults and flaws with compassion.

Because it's kindness that's going to cleanse you.

And compassion that's going to heal you.

There's a fine line between treating yourself with a little tough love—assessing yourself with complete realism and honesty and taking stock of who you are and who you want to become—and tearing yourself apart with a savagely critical eye. The latter way— listening to the voice in your head that says you're bad or you're a failure or you're not worthy of love—is how most people deal with themselves when they want to get tough and start down a path of self-improvement. But what they don't realize is that until they're ready to treat themselves with kindness and compassion and even a sense of humor, they're never really going to feel better.

That harshly judgmental and deeply negative voice in your head has a whole loop of tape filled with all the ways you've failed and done things wrong throughout your life, and that's the voice that has to be silenced if you're ever going to start liking yourself enough to find love.

As I said earlier, you're still the one who has to do the work. This book isn't going to fix everything, but your true journey starts here. The map of that journey has three points on it:

Mind.

Body.

And soul.

With this map, like any other, you have to orient yourself to the basic coordinates. That's what we're going to do now: get a clear understanding of each of these three areas you're going to travel to and then cleanse.

Our first stop is **the mind.**

The mind is purposeful, rational, and capable of deep thought, complex reasoning, and executing one of our most valuable survival and coping strategies: denial.

The mind is our lifelong memory bank, our own personal encyclopedia of knowledge we've acquired through formal education and from life itself, and it's what we use every day to function in all the most fundamental ways. We process what we see, think about what we process, and then make decisions about what we're going to do and how we're going to act based on the information we have.

The mind is also where we form our basic assumptions and impressions of people and situations. It's where our attitudes come from and where our likes and dislikes have a forum to duke it out.

When it comes to dating and the psychology of dating, the mind is the all-important first stop on your trip to that better place inside yourself.

Without addressing your mind—your thoughts and moods and attitudes and goals and preferences—you're going to have far less clarity about the kind of love you're looking for when you really start looking.

The next stop is **the body.**

The body is where most of our "tangibles" exist: that is, the factors that relate to physical appearance and that are most easily changed. People often think that this area is the hardest part of their journey to self-improvement but actually it's the easiest. The tangibles—weight, clothing, style, health, and fitness—are almost always well within our abilities to control.

For dating purposes, the body issue can be divided into two separate parts for us to consider. The first part is whether we are physically healthy. Do we exercise and take care of ourselves because we like ourselves and feel good about ourselves?

The second part of the body question to consider is what we look like: Are we happy with our weight? With how we look in our clothes? With how we wear our hair? Do we generally feel okay when we look in the mirror or do we long for major changes in order to feel better about ourselves as we think about the prospect of looking for—and finding—love?

Tackling both health and appearance requires the understanding that if you really want to find someone you must like yourself.

And the true test of whether you really and truly like yourself is to be able to answer the following question with a yes:

If I introduced you to you, would you be attracted to you?

The third and final stop is the core of our being: **the soul.**

Just the use of the word *soul* is a slightly touchy subject because some people ascribe to the word a religious connotation.

I'm a big believer in being honest about my beliefs, so for me, *soul* is the right word for what I'm talking about when I refer to the inner self that we all have deep inside, past the outer layers of the mind and the body.

For me, the soul goes to a different place when we die.

And for me, the use of the word *soul* to name the almost sacred part of our being—the invisible unknowable part of our being, the most human part of every single one of us and the most divine—isn't necessarily about being religious.

It's about morals and values and ethics.

It's about character and integrity and honesty.

But whether or not you believe in God, whether or not you are a religious person, and whether or not you are a spiritual person, you

THE CORE OF THE CORE

I know this might put some people off but I have a problem with atheists—specifically, clients who come into my office wanting to find love and yet admit to believing in nothing.

I don't care what you believe in. I don't care what religion you are or even if you're part of an organized religion (I myself am a lapsed Catholic); I don't care if you call god "God" or "good energy" or if your "religion" is nature or some other kind of nameless, label-less spiritualism. What I care about is this:

You have to believe in something.

Especially if you want to find love.

If you believe in nothing it means you don't think there's anything bigger than you, or more powerful than you, or more important than you. And that is not only narcissistic; it's negative. That kind of deep and pervasive negativity is a big red flag to me that the person I'm dealing with isn't ready to be matched with anyone because there's anger and hostility at their core.

I find clients who announce to me that they're atheists arrogant, because they're not just saying they don't know if there's a god—however they might define *god*—they're saying they know for sure that God doesn't exist. And there's something about someone *who chooses to believe in nothing* that sets me off.

People don't have to believe in religion. But I believe people need to be spiritual. They need to connect with something bigger than themselves. And they need to choose to believe in something instead of choosing to believe in nothing.

This belief—this spiritual feeling and connection to whatever positive energy feels true to your soul—is the core of the core. The core of your core. Goodness and positive energy have to be rooted there for you to fully enjoy life and find and keep love.

have a core. And that core is the last part of you that needs to be healed and repaired and made healthy and to come alive again—or maybe come alive for the first time ever—in order for you to be truly ready to find love.

CLEANSE CANDIDATE CASE STUDY: MOLLY

I've had thousands of clients who are beleaguered by cripplingly low levels of self-esteem. So when Molly came to see me she didn't set off any alarm bells.

Like many young women I've worked with, Molly had a good job as an office manager for a busy medical practice, lots of friends, and a great, energetic personality. But when she told me that she'd struggled with depression over the last two years I could tell there were going to be some cracks in her façade.

And there were.

I sensed that Molly's soul was burdened with thoughts and concerns and worries that were weighing her down, literally and figuratively: by her own admission she was forty pounds overweight and unhappy about it, and she confessed to being more than a few thousand dollars in credit card debt.

For someone in her mid-twenties she seemed to have a sadness and a heaviness to her soul, and I was determined to find out what was holding back such an attractive and sweet young woman.

As the interview progressed, I learned that Molly had gained her weight following a painful and unexpected breakup with someone she'd been seeing exclusively—or so she thought—for more than a year. Unbeknownst to her, though, her boyfriend had been a true and troubled narcissist who had carried on with other women over the course of their own relationship without her knowing. When Molly finally learned the truth about his deceptive two-timing behavior, she ended the relationship immediately, but not without feeling completely devastated and consumed with self-criticism. She couldn't believe she could ever have been that stupid and not known the true nature of his personality.

During that dark time after the breakup, Molly packed on the pounds. But she gained more than just body weight: she acquired a growing sense of distrust and a gnawing feeling that she wasn't worthy of being loved. Her self-esteem, never exceptionally high, plummeted. She didn't date much, and when she did, she told me that she didn't have much of a libido, something she attributed to her poor self-image because of her weight.

I knew that there was more to Molly's story than just a bad

TANGIBLES AND INTANGIBLES

In life and in dating, there are things that are easy to change and things that aren't as easy. The easiest ones to change I call "tangibles." They are within our control to fix or work on or improve, and they're also easy to pinpoint: they're obvious, clear-cut, and, well, tangible.

Tangibles are things like weight, hair, makeup—almost anything to do with a person's physical appearance and behavior. Most of us have a few tangibles that could stand improvement. Who doesn't wish they could lose a few pounds, firm up their butt, and maybe even be a little less bald?

What's interesting and important about the tangibles in dating terms is that once you improve them, or at least start to improve them, the other less obvious problems you have will automatically improve, too. Not necessarily by 100 percent but enough to see a connection between the obvious and the less obvious aspects of your body and your personality, and to see that with a little work you can truly change yourself and feel better about yourself and increase your chances of eventually finding love.

"Intangibles," then, are things like attitude, mood, and unresolved issues. The list of intangibles is longer than that, of course, but it should be clear from just these few examples that those are the bigger, vaguer, and more difficult things in life to change and fix. Intangibles are like a giant ocean liner—so big that it takes much longer to change course or reverse direction than it takes a small boat to accomplish the same goals.

Most people get hung up on their intangibles. They're overwhelmed by the hugeness of their problems and paralyzed by the fact that they have no idea how to go about making big changes in their life.

But what they don't understand is that they don't always have to make the biggest changes first.

In fact, the best way to start is often with making the smallest and easiest changes. See Chapter 8 for more on how to get started!

breakup and some extra weight. When I asked her about her childhood, she told me that she was only six when her parents went through a messy divorce. The more we talked, the more I began to understand that at Molly's core was an empty place where her fa-

ther had once been—a father who became completely absen.
leaving the marriage and the home. Molly had learned early th.
food and buying things were comforts. Like most of us, she'd fallen
back on those ways in her early adulthood when things got difficult.

But even though Molly knew she had to face her demons—the
sadness and loneliness and anger of the little girl inside her who still
felt abandoned—I realized there was more I needed to do for her besides guiding her in that direction and signing her up for my matchmaking services.

Molly needed a different kind of intervention.

She needed a mind/body/soul cleanse.

Molly's Cleanse: Making a List

Once I realized Molly was going to need a different sort of approach—something more than my usual intervention-style interview—I made an even more concentrated effort to get to her core.
That's not always easy to do in the relatively short time I have with
a client. After all, therapists and psychiatrists can spend hours and
even years with patients before getting to their deepest issues. But
my questions are targeted to give me specific information for the
purpose of dating: information that's going to help me figure out a
client as quickly as possible so that I can come up with a practical
strategy to help them as quickly as possible.

Because the faster I can help them get over themselves, the faster
I can help them find love.

Luckily, Molly wanted my help and she was open, honest, and
forthcoming with her answers. This is a crucial factor in the process,
of course: whether the person I'm trying to help truly wants to be
helped and is willing to bare their thoughts and feelings to me.
Sometimes it's why the intervention process breaks down at this
early stage. Some people, for whatever reasons, just aren't ready for
the help they think they want, and their unwillingness or inability to
open up fully is a deal breaker.

I can't change someone who doesn't want to change.

But Molly was one of those clients who was ready, and so we
forged ahead and made a great deal of progress in a short time.

The first thing I did after I'd gotten a sense of Molly in the broadest strokes was to make a list of the issues I thought we needed to focus on:

1. *Money Was on Her Mind.* One of the biggest issues preying on Molly's mind was money: she was in debt and couldn't seem to manage her finances well enough to stay on a budget.

2. *Weight Was Weighing Her Down.* Molly was very unhappy with her body and knew that losing weight was key to getting some of her self-esteem back.

3. *Sadness Was Sucking the Life Out of Her Soul.* The deep sadness that Molly had suffered as a child had taken its toll on Molly as an adult, and she knew that if she was ever going to have a truly healthy and happy relationship with a man she would have to get over her feelings of abandonment.

First Stop: Molly's Mind

Unlike some people, who are unemployed or have unsteady incomes, Molly had a solid, steady income, so her earning ability wasn't the problem. The problem was being careless with the money she earned and not being realistic about what she could and could not afford.

Money (and how to spend it) is one of the most common problems people have, and it's an especially common problem for couples, which is why it's critical that people address their own financial issues by themselves before they enter into a relationship with another person and things really get complicated. If you understand and identify your own personal financial issues and solve them now, when you're still single—and when you're still able to have full and complete control of your money—you'll save yourself a huge amount of misery and unhappiness down the road.

It was clear that Molly needed help with her money. Whether with me, now, or with a professional financial planner at some future point, she needed to have a dialogue about her finances and come up with a realistic budget that she could stick to in order to get herself out of debt and prevent her from racking up more credit card charges.

The solution to dealing with a problem like Molly's with money is to sit down and face the situation, just as we did in the "Facing Your Demons" chapter. This might sound completely obvious and overly simplistic but often the reason people can't solve their problem is because they can't even bear to think about it, let alone try to fix it.

In Molly's case, I told her that when she went home I wanted her to make a list of her bills. I wanted her to look at that list, and then I wanted her to look at her paycheck stub and write down the amount of money she was bringing in every month.

And once she had looked at her bills and added up the amount of money she spent every month, and after she'd compared that number to the amount of money she earned every month, I wanted her to think about ways she could cut her spending so that she could start living within her means.

This, I told her, was called a budget.

And in order for her to get over her money issues and cleanse her mind of all the worry and concern it was burdening her with, she was going to have to follow that budget as best she could.

Second Stop: Molly's Body

The obvious focus of the body phase of Molly's cleanse was diet. A plan of healthy eating and regular exercise would let Molly begin to lose weight and, simultaneously, to regain some self-esteem. Her goal to start, I suggested, shouldn't be some unrealistically low number on the scale, but to get within twenty pounds of her ideal weight.

It's amazing how quickly positive energy can replace negative energy. Just ask anyone who loses the first five pounds on a diet—almost instantly a person's mood improves, their energy increases, and a newfound sense of hope is suddenly apparent. I knew that the minute Molly started losing weight, she would start to feel less burdened and more and more positive about herself and her future.

Weight, like so many other issues people have in their daily life and in their dating life, is a symptom: a symptom of a larger issue or conflict. For Molly, her weight was a symptom of her low self-esteem—how bad she felt about herself after discovering her boyfriend had been cheating on her all along, and how bad she felt most of her life after her parents' divorce because she missed her dad and felt abandoned by him.

Wounds like those don't disappear overnight, but clarifying those issues and understanding her depression and why she'd gained the weight was a huge step in the cleansing process, and it would make the rest of the journey possible.

Last Stop: Molly's Soul

Just as we'd discovered when we were focusing on Molly's body issues, we found that self-esteem—or, more exactly, low self-esteem—was at the deep core of Molly's soul. She didn't like herself very much, and she hadn't had much success with relationships. Before the deceptive cheater, she'd had relationships with guys she knew early on weren't keepers. They were guys she never truly connected with and who never made her feel special and because of that, she began to realize, she hadn't felt strong chemistry with any of them.

Molly knew that one of the things she wanted most in life was to find someone she had that chemistry with, someone she would feel deeply connected to. I knew if she wanted those things she was going to have to do things every day to boost her self-esteem.

She was going to have to do things every day that would make her feel like a special person, an attractive person, a person worthy of love.

She was going to have to get over the pain caused by her parents' divorce that she felt as a child. Rejection by her father was a huge part of that pain, so it was crucial for Molly to try to understand as the adult she is now that her father may have stopped loving her mother and her mother may have stopped loving him, but they hadn't stopped loving her. In order to get over that big demon—rejection—she was going to have to separate the pain in her past from the reality of the present.

Part of the reality of Molly's present and a result of the rejection she had felt was that she got mad very easily. All that old unresolved anger that she kept inside would frequently surface. It was a feeling and a behavior she didn't like and wanted very much to change, and I had a perfect plan for how she could do that.

Cleansing the mind and the body and the soul is one thing: we rid ourselves of all the negative energy and associations and behaviors that burden us. But once those things are gone and we've cleared out the bad feelings and the pain and the sadness and the losses we've suffered, we need to fill that space with something new.

We need to fill that new clean space inside ourselves with kindness: kindness toward ourselves, and kindness toward others.

This final step of the cleanse is really important because it gives you some concrete ways to put into practice the concepts we've been talking about so far: how to make changes in your life that make you feel good and lead you toward finding happiness and finding love.

To help Molly make those changes, I gave her a simple three-step self-esteem boosting prescription that you too can follow:

1. *Change your computer password to something that reminds you every day that you love yourself.* Okay, well, you don't have to change your password to "ILoveMe"—I wouldn't want every single person who reads this book to have the same computer password and get their computers hacked—but change it to something self-affirming. This one simple act will reinforce your commitment to learning how to love yourself, and soon the act of practicing it every day will pay off and actual self-love will follow.

2. *Do something kind for someone every day.* There's a biblical word I use for this—*tithing*—because it captures the true essence of this action: human kindness and generosity. Loosely defined, tithing is the act of sharing one's abundance with others. Doing good for and sharing your strength with someone, anyone, every day—whether with a coworker or another driver on the road or an elderly person crossing the street—will make you feel connected to humanity, and that feeling of goodness and kindness and generosity and connection will feed your soul and heal you on a very deep level.

3. *Look for the life lessons hiding in your experiences.* If you go through your life ignoring the lessons you're supposed to learn from each and every experience you have, good or bad, you'll have to face each lesson over and over and over again until you learn it. It's our job to learn these lessons—to learn from our mistakes, to learn how to survive our lives and get over the things that have stopped us from feeling truly happy and alive. Seeing what you need to see, changing what you need to change, and understanding that in order to find love you need to face all the things you need to face is the crucial last step in the cleansing process.

Sometimes even when we look very hard, we can't see what we need to see; looking for life lessons and finding them are two separate things. Sometimes it takes a third party—me as a matchmaker or another kind of help—to see the things that are holding you back. See the Resources appendix at the back of this book for places that can help you get to your core and help you discover what you need to see and learn to move forward with your search for love.

7

The Keys to Successful Relationships

That Most People Have Lost, Misplaced,
or Never Had to Begin With

In this "Getting to Your Core" section of the book, we've done some of the hardest work in the process of getting yourself emotionally, physically, and spiritually ready to find love.

We've talked about the all-important need to face your demons so that you can start to resolve some of the most painful issues in your past and move beyond them into your future.

We've addressed the empty space created when those demons are gone, and how to truly heal the three layers of your being—mind, body, and soul—that were affected by those demons.

Now we're at the last stage of the work we're going to do with the core.

Our focus is going to be on the three most crucial and basic and fundamental keys to healthy relationships—dating or otherwise:

Common sense.

Self-esteem.

And kindness.

A lot of what we cover in this book is, on the most obvious level, related to dating and finding love, but almost everything we talk about that goes into having healthy and successful romantic relationships also goes into having all kinds of healthy and successful relationships: with friends and family, with colleagues and coworkers, even with ourselves.

We've talked too, in previous chapters, about some of the more superficial problems that people frequently blame their dating troubles on—namely, issues having to do with their appearance, like weight and attractiveness—but sometimes their biggest problem has nothing to do with those things. Sometimes, their biggest problem is that they have a significant lack of one or all of the qualities of common sense, self-esteem, and kindness.

Because without enough of these qualities—let alone without *any* of them—you're not going to get very far in finding, or keeping, love.

THE IMPORTANCE OF COMMON SENSE

To me, common sense is one of the most important qualities a person can have. And in my experience, it's also one trait that many people don't have.

Common sense is becoming more and more uncommon, and because of that inverse equation, people are having a lot more trouble finding love.

Common sense isn't taught in school and it isn't about being educated or book smart. But in the same way that some people have to work hard to get good grades and other people have the gift of doing well in school, some people have to work hard at learning common sense. Which really means that they have to learn to pay attention, since so much of common sense is being alert and aware of your surroundings and of what people around you are saying and doing.

I've often wondered when and why people lost their common sense, why so many people these days have trouble understanding the most basic concepts concerning general human behavior, and why, if there was a test in Life 101, they would almost certainly fail it.

My parents taught me about common sense very early in my life and suggested strongly over the years that I call on it when the time came to make the decisions and choices I was faced with.

To this day I remember being taught the most basic things in everyday life: how to dress for the snow (especially important growing up in Buffalo, New York) and for work, for first dates, and for formal events and occasions.

They taught me the simple rules of sitting at a table and eating dinner: what to do with my napkin, which silverware to use first, the correct way to use a knife and fork.

Most important, they taught me manners: how to speak properly, how to behave in the company of others, how to treat people with respect and kindness, and how important it is to say *please* and *thank you*. You might think these are issues of etiquette but because they are so fundamental to having successful human interactions, I think of them absolutely as matters of common sense.

There are countless other examples of small bits of simple wisdom my parents taught me directly or showed me through their actions and their words, knowledge about life and how the world works and how best to get along in it. I have always felt lucky to have been raised in that environment, a home where parents were parents and kids were kids, and where the hierarchy was clear: the adults had lessons to teach and the children knew they had lessons to learn.

Common sense gets you through life, and a lack of common sense can really get in the way of dating. More clients than you can imagine have a significant deficiency in this area, and that deficiency is a big handicap for them when it comes to their social interactions and romantic relationships.

Some people were never taught the basics of Life 101 or have forgotten what little they learned, and there are many seemingly simple situations that the commonsense-challenged person will stumble over.

I'll be honest: I tend to get very frustrated with clients who have little or no common sense. Maybe you wouldn't blame me if you had my job and heard the stories I do about people with no common sense whatsoever.

Why else would they show up for a first date wearing a pink top hat, or a sweatshirt and sweatpants, or a wrinkled button-down shirt, or a shirt that makes a 38-DD bust look like a 48-DDD, or jeans that are three sizes too small?

Why else would they talk about their sex life, past or present, or their finances, or their sad, sorry stories about their childhood or their first marriages, or why they hate their ex?

Why else would they wipe their nose on their jacket?

Or not clean out the two months' worth of fast food wrappers from their car before they drive their date home?

Or talk about the twenty-two cats they have?

Or how they wish they could live with their mother for the rest of their life?

Why else would they ask their dates questions they themselves don't want to answer?

Or have expectations for who they want to meet that far exceed their own limitations?

Or talk about how independent they are and how they don't need a man when they're sitting across from one on a first date?

When clients expect me to solve all their problems in one month when they've been alone for fifteen years, I tell them this:

Get over yourself! I'm a matchmaker, not a magician!

Sometimes clients with extreme cases of adult ignorance can't be helped.

But most people can be helped in one way or another with a refresher course in common sense. Usually that's enough to improve their basic people skills and get them to reenter the dating world without blowing it.

No matter how much I wish I could make dating sound like rocket science, it isn't.

Dating is about common sense.

And about understanding human nature and human behavior at their most basic and elemental levels.

I always tell clients that I don't make the rules, I just follow them. When it comes to matters related to common sense, that couldn't be more true.

We'll get into the actual specifics of dating do's and don'ts in the next part of the book, but for now, I'll lay out the most basic com-

FIVE BASIC COMMONSENSE DATING PRINCIPLES

1. **Too much information is a turnoff.** Some people shorten this to "TMI," but whatever you call it, don't talk too much about personal or sensitive topics. Spilling your guts—or hearing someone spill theirs—is a huge turnoff.

2. **Less is more, especially when it comes to clothing, makeup, and showing skin.** To prove this point my father used to tell me to think of that famous photograph of Marilyn Monroe in a black turtleneck—sexy without showing any skin below her chin. You can still be attractive and sexy without showing up for a date practically naked.

3. **Lay off the alcohol.** Staying sober is the most obvious way to keep your wits about you. Dating, especially in the early stages, requires you to pick up cues and process information about what the other person is saying or doing, and make judgment calls about your safety and well-being, both physical and emotional.

4. **Keep your objective in mind.** Remember that dating is about attracting the other person, not turning them off or repelling them or freaking them out or scaring them off. Think about this when you are considering wearing that piano key tie from 1986, or slathering on some pancake makeup, or applying that fifth coat of mascara, or confessing that you haven't kissed anyone in ten years.

5. **Know your dating weaknesses and try to prepare for them.** If you're someone who takes forever to get ready for a date because you try on every single thing in your closet, then be sure to leave yourself plenty of extra time to get dressed instead of racing out the door half-ready or showing up late. If you're someone who is painfully shy or has trouble making small talk, have a few topics in mind to talk about, and read the paper or watch the news so you'll be able to engage in some intelligent conversation about current events. If you have trouble remembering names, say your date's name ten times before you see him or her so that it rolls off your tongue without your having to worry about it.

monsense rules to follow if you want to improve your dating skills and your chances of finding love.

MY SEEMINGLY-OBVIOUS-BUT-OBVIOUSLY-NOT-OBVIOUS COMMONSENSE RULES FOR IMPROVING YOUR DATING COMMON SENSE (A PARTIAL LIST)

- Dress appropriately for meeting someone new. Remember that just as with job interviews, appearance and first impressions count. This means no sweats, no wrinkled or ripped or dirty clothes, no clothes that are three sizes too small or that show your butt crack or your tramp stamp, no blouses or tank tops where cleavage or bra straps are hanging out. If you feel that this is going to be a problem, you can put the book down right now.
- Do not get drunk on a first date. Or a second date, for that matter. Or let's just say that passing out or dancing on a table or doing anything else inappropriate with someone you're just getting to know isn't going to get you very far. In fact, drinking too much too soon will almost certainly red-flag you, and if it doesn't then your date probably doesn't have very good judgment, either. For those of you who are unclear about what "drinking too much" means, assume that doing shots should be off your list. As for beer, wine, and mixed drinks, make sure you have something in your stomach before you start drinking. Then set a limit of two drinks before switching to soft drinks or bubbly water.
- Don't talk about money—how much you have, how much you make, how much you owe. Your date should not walk away from your first meeting knowing your balance sheet. And don't ask questions about your date's finances, either. This rule includes not complaining about how overpriced a restaurant's menu is or how expensive you think the bill is (even if they are). Cheapness, or even just the mistaken impression of cheapness, is unattractive.
- Be polite. There's nothing more unattractive than someone who is rude to others—especially to waiters and waitresses. Since most first dates and second dates take place in a bar or restaurant, make sure you watch your manners. Say *please* and *thank you* and if you're dissatisfied with the service or with your food, either express yourself politely or eat it—literally.

- Watch your table manners. This might seem ridiculous even to mention, but how you eat and even what you eat on a first or second date can make or break you. Besides the obvious—using your knife and fork correctly and putting your napkin on your lap as opposed to wearing it as a bib—there are things like slurping your food or chewing with your mouth open or not realizing there's a crouton stuck in your beard. Don't eat with your fingers unless you have to and don't, under any circumstances, lick your fingers. Also, if you're working on your weight and have mentioned that to your date, don't sit down and order fettuccine Alfredo and a loaf of garlic bread and a giant sundae for dessert, because common sense will tell your date that you're not working on your weight.

- Don't talk about sex for the first few dates. Don't talk about all the sex you've had. And don't talk about all the sex you haven't had. No one needs to know this much about you this early on.

- Don't talk about medication you're on or any diseases you have. If you take antidepressants, for instance, your date doesn't need to know it the first time you have dinner. If you have a sexually transmitted disease, it's inappropriate to discuss that unless you're planning on sleeping with that person. Remember that for the first few dates, these people are essentially strangers to you, so don't tell them anything you wouldn't tell someone you barely know.

- Don't tell the sad sorry tale of your underactive or nonexistent love life. Not only does it fall into the too-much-information category, but it also will inevitably cast you in a negative light. Keep the conversation light and positive and steer away from very personal subject matter and complaints about exes or past relationships.

THE IMPORTANCE OF SELF-ESTEEM

This is one of those statements that always sound like the inside of a greeting card, but I can't think of many things more true: If you don't love yourself, no one else will.

The reason we're talking about self-esteem so much in this book is because without it, you will never find love.

Without it, you will never attract someone who truly loves you because you haven't been able to attract and win over the most important person out there:

You.

How can you expect someone else to love you—your flaws and your weaknesses and your mistakes and your failings—if you don't?

How can you expect someone else to love you—your chubby thighs or too short legs or too bald head or too big nose—if you don't?

How can you expect someone else to love you—all parts of you, the good, the bad, and the ugly—when you don't love yourself?

Like common sense, self-esteem and self-love—the offshoots of which are self-confidence and a healthy ego—are usually developed at home, imparted by parents who make their children feel loved and safe and cared for in all ways from a very early age. Basic needs—food, shelter, human touch, and affection—have to be met for a child to feel that deep love and safety, and without them, they will bear the scars of those deficits forever. A baby who isn't held and comforted when she cries, a child who doesn't have his tears wiped away and get a hug when he feels scared or sad or sick or lost, a teen who is hurt by words or harsh punishment or physical abuse or who is ignored completely, becomes an adult who is wounded, broken in places they can't see and don't know how to fix.

Kids who grow up without enough love or kindness end up missing something else very important: the ability to treat their broken hearts and wounded souls with compassion.

And without compassion, they can never heal.

There are few absolutes in this world, but one of them is that if you don't heal, if you continue to live your life feeling the raw pain of all the hurt you've suffered, you will never feel truly happy. You will never be able to put the past behind you and move forward because you will always and forever assume that being hurt is your destiny, that somehow it is your fault and your doing, and that for whatever reasons and in whatever ways, you are attracting your own misfortune.

I don't know of a single child or a single person who was emotionally or verbally or physically abused about whom it could be said that the abuse was their fault.

Because it wasn't.

With dating, though, responsibility comes into play, and the question of victimhood and choice becomes much more cloudy.

Adults who date have control of their destiny. They have control over the types of people they choose to go out with, choose to go home with, choose to sleep with, choose to marry.

Adults have control over the sort of life they want to lead, or at least, want to try to lead, and who they want to lead it with.

Which is why this part of the process of getting over yourself is so crucial.

Unless you are ready for the good guy, the good person, the good relationship, you will probably continue attracting, and being attracted to, negative people and relationships.

I've had clients who, when I've asked them if they were ready for the good guy, the good relationship, the good person who is going to treat them the way they deserve to be treated, have said, "Yes, I'm ready."

And so we've moved forward in the process of finding them love.

I've also had clients who, when I asked them that same question, have either said they were ready when they weren't, or admitted that no, they weren't ready.

And they have stood up and left my office.

I don't go after people who leave my office and try to bring them back, even if I want to. A person has to be ready for my help before I can help them.

Some of them eventually come back when they're ready, finally, to change their fortune, ready to believe enough in their self-worth to meet different people and make different choices—healthier people and healthier choices.

And coming back, taking that first step, is more than half the battle in finding love.

If you're reading this now, unsure of whether or not you yourself are ready for the good guy, the good relationship, the good person who is going to treat you the way you truly deserve to be treated— with love and respect and like the special treasure that you are—I hope you will take this first step.

I hope you will feel ready for the good thing.

And I hope you keep reading and searching deep inside yourself

---

THE ONE QUESTION SELF-ESTEEM TEST

I could ask you twenty questions to see if you have a problem with self-esteem—how low your self-esteem is and why you think you feel so bad about yourself—but instead, I'm just going to ask you one question. It's a question I frequently ask clients because it perfectly encapsulates how they feel about themselves while also getting them to think about the issues they're going to need to address in order to have more success with dating and to eventually find love:

If I introduced you to you, would you want to date you?

---

and doing the work you need to do so that you will be ready to find love.

And keep it.

THE IMPORTANCE OF KINDNESS

The third and final key to finding love and keeping it is kindness.

When I say this to some people they look surprised. They're thinking that a hot bod and a big bank account are the real keys to finding love.

Kindness is one of those words that sound old-fashioned these days because, like many other core values, being kind to people has become an outdated concept. Those of us raised in the "Me" generation and all of us living in the current "I" generation are no longer conditioned to think of what we can do to help others. We're conditioned now to think only of ourselves: our music, our laptops, our giant SUVs.

I said in the previous chapter that one of the ways to feed your soul is to do one good thing for someone every single day. This act—the act of tithing—is one way of putting into daily practice the idea that we have to think of the needs and well-being of others, not just our own.

As it turns out, when it comes to dating, kindness is an extremely important idea for a very simple reason:

Without kindness, how are you going to sit across from someone you've just met and barely know and are thinking of dating and have any chance of accepting their limitations and imperfections?

Without kindness, how are you going to get past the issues, big and small, that people have to get past in order to connect?

Dating is about a lot of things—common sense, knowing how to make conversation, and learning how to dress and present yourself physically in the best possible light, to name only a few skills that we're covering here in this book and that are the basic building blocks to successfully meeting people and having the chance to form relationships. But without kindness in the mix, none of these skills will be enough to turn your dating situation around. Self-improvement skills rarely focus on the idea of kindness, of understanding, of human compassion and acceptance, of compromise. But these are ideas that have to be present in your mind and in your heart when you go out there and start meeting people. Because if you have none of these thoughts in your head or feelings in your heart, if instead you are filled with judgment and criticism and an inflexible set of conditions and rules and attributes that you're looking for in a partner, you will walk away from every date feeling disappointed.

You will reject people before they deserve to be rejected.

You will walk away from the opportunity to learn more about a person before deciding they are not for you.

You will deprive yourself of the chance of connecting with someone who might actually be a great match for you.

And you will do all those things because you don't have the kindness to give the new person across from you at least the benefit of the doubt.

Which means taking more than five seconds to decide whether or not your date is the one for you.

Walking into a date with kindness in your heart does not mean agreeing to date or going home with every Tom, Dick, or Harry that you meet. It doesn't mean you should ignore your gut feelings or that you should lower your standards on character or integrity or honesty. And it doesn't mean that you have to stand for rude or disrespectful behavior.

That's not what I mean by being kind.

The kindness I'm talking about is a larger kindness—generosity of spirit, acceptance and compassion for other people's flaws.

MY GOLDEN RULES FOR DATING

- If you decide you don't want to see someone for a second date, you should let that person know, in as kind a way possible, and not leave them hanging by not returning phone messages or e-mails or texts.
- If you are bored in a relationship and feel it's not working, you should be straightforward and honest and leave the relationship cleanly, without cheating or hurting the person because you're too chicken to face the situation directly and end it.
- If you have had your heart broken by someone—and we all have—don't go and break someone else's heart. Don't be as careless with someone else's feelings and emotions as someone was with yours. If you're going to spend months or years crying about how you've been hurt and treated badly, you'd better not turn around and do the same thing. Remember that two wrongs don't make a right.
- If you want to be accepted for who you are—warts and all—try accepting someone else for who *they* are. All too often the biggest complainers about being harshly judged by others and about feeling rejected because of their flaws are the worst and harshest rejecters themselves.
- Don't lie, embellish, stretch the truth, or misrepresent yourself in any way to people you want to date. Not only is dishonesty bad karma, but you will eventually get caught. If the fear of getting caught isn't enough to scare you straight, think of how tricked and mistrustful you would feel if you found out the person you were getting to know was stretching the truth and telling you a pack of lies.
- Remember that the Golden Rule applies to all your dealings with people—not only the ones you're dating or hoping to date. You should be treating everyone in your life—at home, at work, in the supermarket, on the highway—with the same kindness and respect with which you want them to treat you.
- Remember, too, that the Golden Rule applies to all your dealings with Internet dating. Just because you can't see the person you're "talking" to and flirting with in e-mails and text messages doesn't mean that they don't have feelings. If you get to a point in your virtual relationship where you decide you're not interested in going farther, let them know as directly and with as much kindness as possible before you move on.

> • Understand that being honest doesn't mean being hurtful or cruel. Think about what you're going to say to someone before you say it and figure out how to get your message across as carefully and constructively as possible by imagining what it would feel like for you to hear what you're about to tell them.

Enough to at least end the date with honesty and straightforwardness and good manners—all of which are rarely seen in modern dating.

I'm a big believer in karma—the idea that what goes around comes around. With dating, in moments in life in which people make themselves emotionally vulnerable and expose the most fragile part of themselves—their hearts—this couldn't be more true. Which is why I tell clients that they should treat people the way they want to be treated, and why I'm telling you, the reader, the same thing.

Part Three

almost
over it

Tangibles and Intangibles

Changing What You Can, Toning Down What You Can't, and Watching Everything Else Fall Into Place

Like scuba divers, we went way, way down into our core in the last section, and now it's time to come back up to the surface, and take a breath. Diving down into your core isn't easy, and the energy, will, and courage it takes to think about the topics we covered in those tough chapters isn't easy, either.

But who said getting over yourself was going to be easy?

I certainly didn't!

Anything worth having is worth working hard for, right? So let's keep going so I can do my job and help you find love.

Now that we're back to the surface—your surface, your outer self—we're going to focus on the tangibles, the aspects of your appearance or behavior that have caused you difficulties with dating and relationships in the past. A tangible is like the tip of an iceberg: it's an issue that you can see and point to as being related to the problems you're having with dating. It's also usually the obvious and visible symptom of bigger core issues that lie beneath your surface—issues you're going to have to get to and work on and face.

THINGS THAT ARE (RELATIVELY) EASY TO CHANGE
VS. THINGS THAT ARE NOT

Not everything you need to work on for the purpose of dating is buried deep in your core, though of course that's where the roots of your primary issues reside.

Most of the things you're going to need to think about and look at and work on—and eventually change and improve—as you get ready to get out there and start successfully dating are things that are closer to the surface or even right on the surface: things that you can see and readily identify as negatives and that you want to turn into positives.

I call these visible and readily identifiable things tangibles, because that's what they are. They're aspects of how you present yourself to the world—your looks and your attitudes and your habits of daily life—that you can point to as being contributing factors to why you're having trouble connecting with new people.

They're also tangible because not only can you see them, but I can see them.

Which means the people you're meeting and dating—or hoping to date—can see them, too.

Unlike core issues, which are convoluted and complicated and never entirely clear, tangibles are obvious. They're the giant elephants in the room: you can't miss them.

For instance, when someone walks into my office who weighs more than three hundred pounds, I'd be an idiot if I didn't register the fact that he or she has a weight problem. Likewise, when a person dressed like a slob comes in, it's clear they have grooming issues. And when a person wearing enough makeup for three clowns comes in, it's obvious that not only are they cosmetically challenged, but probably they have some issues with reality, too. Here are some common tangible issues:

- Being overweight
- In need of grooming (hair, nails, teeth, hair removal)
- Too much makeup
- No makeup
- Too tough looking

- Too tan
- Too much cleavage showing
- Clothing that's wrinkled, out of style, ill-fitting, or inappropriate
- Haircut that's outdated, overprocessed, or overstyled
- Speaking inappropriately (using bad grammar, foul language)
- Nervous talking, overtalking, or interrupting
- Difficulty making conversation
- No eye contact
- Self-absorbed and self-centered conversational topics
- Too self-deprecating
- Bitchy, bitter, critical, or complaining
- Needy, insecure, or desperate

Some tangibles aren't immediately apparent, but they become clear through the interview process or when I talk to clients after their dates to get feedback on the person I've set them up with and to get feedback from the other person on them. They also surface during actual dates and are picked up and noticed by the person you're out with. These less obvious but still tangible tangibles would include:

Issues with money (cheapness)

Financial problems (debt, living above their means)

Excessive smoking or drinking (or other substance abuse)

Messiness of home or car

Single mom or dad who can't get out of "parent" mode

Rudeness to waiters/waitresses

Too flirtatious with others who are not their dates

Won't stop the booty calls

Pathological pickiness

■ Trouble with relationships with family, friends, children, coworkers

■ Emotional problems (depression, anger management)

■ Obsessed with ex-wife/husband or ex-boyfriend/girlfriend

■ Still getting over a breakup or divorce

■ Boring in bed

You'll notice that some of these less obvious tangibles overlap with some of the garage door behaviors outlined in Chapter 4, and that's because tangible problems and behaviors develop and strengthen over time to protect us from being vulnerable. Which means that behind the weight problem, or the sloppy appearance, or the clown makeup are bigger issues: core issues that cause the tangibles.

Intangibles are the same core issues that we discussed in the last chapter. They're the larger, deeper problems that are the true cause of visible problematic behavior, and they are almost always the source of several tangible offshoots.

A few examples of intangibles would include:

• Low self-esteem
• Trust issues
• Intimacy issues
• Sadness, depression, and pessimism
• Anger issues
• Low self-confidence
• Unresolved relationship issues (divorce, breakup)
• Unresolved childhood issues (divorce, abuse)
• Sexual problems (no, low, or overactive libido)

For instance, when someone has a weight problem, they usually have a few other issues, too, that are related to their weight and self-image: maybe they wear ill-fitting clothes, or they don't wear any

FIG. 1. THE RELATIONSHIP BETWEEN TANGIBLES AND INTANGIBLES—WEIGHT

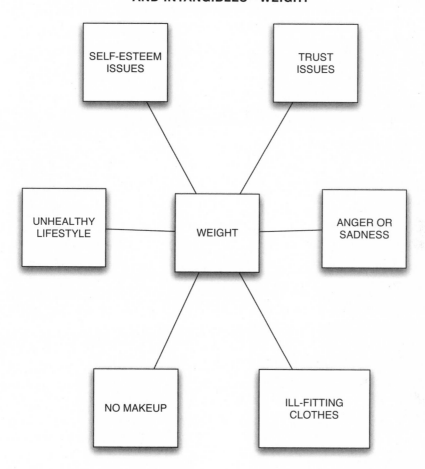

makeup, or they don't exercise or take care of their health. These secondary issues, in turn, can be traced back to at least one intangible, if not more, creating something that can actually be drawn, as in the flow chart above.

Now let's get more specific. Let's go back to Molly from Chapter 6. The main problem she felt was keeping her back from dating—keeping her from going out and feeling attractive and having a healthy libido—was her weight.

FIG. 2. MOLLY'S CHART OF TANGIBLES AND INTANGIBLES

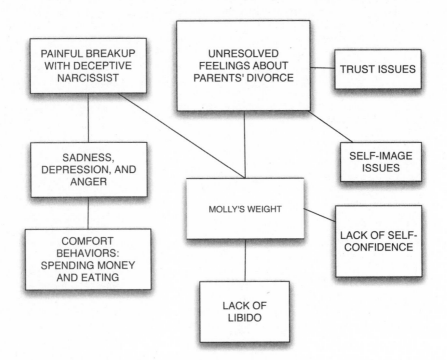

So her weight gain is a tangible. But the cause of that weight gain is an intangible: her weight gain had been brought on by the painful ending of her relationship with a deceptive narcissist.

And that intangible leads to more intangibles.

The hurt she felt from that experience tapped into the older hurt she was still carrying around from childhood: her parents' divorce and the sadness she felt over the loss of her father's presence in her life.

That hurt undermined her self-esteem, which led to a lack of self-confidence and a general sadness and depression.

She had learned that food and shopping alleviated that sadness and depression.

But that in turn led to her weight problem and her significant credit card debt and problems with budgeting her money.

So, if we were to map Molly's tangibles and intangibles, her chart would look like the one on the previous page.

SMALL TANGIBLE CHANGES = BIG INTANGIBLE CHANGES

Clients usually feel that making changes to their appearance or modifying their behavior is the hardest part of the process of finding love, but I always tell them that it is actually the easiest part. If you make some small changes—for example, lose ten pounds of the forty you ultimately want to shed and get a new haircut and a makeover while you're waiting for the weight to come off—you'll immediately start to feel better about yourself. And that change in attitude will fuel the rest of your journey.

Let's go over some of the other common tangibles and how you can improve on them, and how those improvements will begin to positively affect your intangibles.

TANGIBLE PROBLEM #1: GENERAL APPEARANCE PROBLEMS

All too often I've suggested that a potential client change something about their appearance, only to be told that they're happy with the way they look.

But your look's not working for you! I'll tell them.

I'll also tell them that we live in a physical world. You have ten seconds to make an impression—good or bad—so it's important that you look your best. Even though I advise clients to give the people they're meeting more than that first ten seconds—to give them at least a half an hour to see the true person behind the imperfect hair or clothes or shoes—the reality is that visual impressions, especially for men, are very powerful. We're not talking about perfection here—the world is full of average and average is okay. But we *are* talking about improving your look so that if you want a second date with someone you can have one. Most people with appearance issues other than weight seem oddly unaware of their less than ideal look. They don't mind their own outdated big eighties hair, bad shoes, nails that are too long, clothes that are too big or too small or just plain unflattering and unstylish. Middle-aged "eccentric" women, wannabe-rock-star guys, and everyone in between, including excessive cleavage showers and tanners and makeup wearers, and men who are so underdressed for dates they won't be allowed into a decent restaurant are all candidates for appearance-related interventions.

Suggestion for Improvement:
Consult Friends or Makeover Professionals

Fixes to your appearance don't need to cost a fortune, though it's worth investing as much as you can comfortably afford on good basics—a good haircut, a few good pieces of clothing, a good handbag and shoes, and going to see someone who can teach you how to dress or apply makeup so that it flatters you and highlights your best features while downplaying your less than ideal features. A few hours with someone who really knows about fashion and color and style can make a huge difference in your success rate as you start going out on dates. If weight and fitness are holding you back from maximizing your looks, start a sensible weight-loss program. Begin walking every day if you can't afford to join a gym or think you won't have time to use it. As for clothes and hair and makeup, while consulting professionals can be very helpful, consulting friends can help, too. Almost everyone knows someone who has great style and knows a lot about clothes and fashion, someone who can take you under their wing and get you started on the road to looking better. Don't be shy about asking for their opinion and help. Sometimes arranging your own intervention is a great way to take charge and make some quick and crucial changes to your look.

Positive Effect on Intangibles: Making some quick changes to your appearance will instantly and significantly affect how you feel about yourself. This will go to your core issues of self-image, self-esteem, and self-confidence. It will jump-start your sense of yourself as an attractive person who is worthy of love. It will even improve your libido. While self-acceptance is a great thing—being realistic about certain physical limitations of your body in general and aging in particular (like your stretch marks, crow's feet, and gray hair roots) is fabulous and one of the hallmarks of a truly happy and content person—there are times when change and improvement is a good thing. And getting ready to date is one of those times.

TANGIBLE PROBLEM #2: TALKING TOO MUCH

This is one of the most common tangibles I see in my office or hear about secondhand through clients who have gone on dates with people who talk too much. There's nothing very convoluted or hidden here: you're just talking way too much, which can overwhelm and annoy your date. Talking too much also means that you're not listening to your date because, obviously, you're too busy talking, and that can be boring and annoying, too. At some point, say during the second hour of you not letting your date get a word in edgewise, they're going to be completely turned off and decide against ever having a second date with you.

Suggestion for Improvement: Work on Your Communication Skills

Talking too much falls into the communication skills subset of tangibles and, assuming you have a garden-variety issue with overtalking (as opposed to something truly pathological), you can, with practice and some very basic tips, improve on this fairly easily. Practice your listening skills with a friend. Have them tell you to shut up when you start talking too much or when you interrupt them. Start to become keenly aware of how much you're talking and how much you're listening. If you're a nervous talker meditate before a date so that you can try to relax. Come up with a list of questions to ask your date—not interrogation questions, but simple, friendly ones that will help you learn more about the person you're talking to. Ask them about their work, their hobbies, what they like to do on the weekends, what kind of music they're into. Asking questions will force you to stop talking and to listen—assuming you can get your interrupting problem under control, too.

Positive Effect on Intangibles: The more you improve your ability to communicate, the less you will totally turn off the people you're trying to attract. Learning to listen to others will help you with your social anxiety issues, narcissistic tendencies, and any habitual one-upping, bragging, or showing off. That need to impress—to show off, to convince your date that you are great—is a big red flag for deep insecurity. The more you control these self-aggrandizing urges, the more people will be able to actually like you for who you are, *instead of who you're telling them you are.* Remember that less is more—in this case, less talking and more listening.

TANGIBLE PROBLEM #3: POOR EYE CONTACT

It always makes me uncomfortable when I see a client for the first time and they won't meet my eyes. A person who doesn't make eye contact somehow seems untrustworthy and dishonest, even if they're neither of those things, because we feel uneasy around someone who won't look at us directly. Making eye contact with another person is one of the most basic ways you can let another person read you, and it's also one of the most basic aspects of flirting—neither of which can happen if you keep averting your eyes and looking at everything and everyone except the person sitting across from you.

Suggestion for Improvement: Practice With a Friend

Once again, working with a friend can do wonders for your eye contact. Ask your friend to tell you when you are looking away and to remind you to stop. With enough practice, you'll raise your awareness enough to really improve in this area, which will help you be much more successful when you're out there dating.

Positive Effect on Intangibles: The more you improve your social skills, the more comfortable you'll feel in social situations. And the more comfortable you feel, the more successful you'll be when you're in them. This will obviously improve your issues with confidence and self-esteem and even help improve your mood, since human contact and communication will make you feel less lonely and isolated within yourself.

TANGIBLE PROBLEM #4: SHYNESS AND NERVOUSNESS

We touched on the issue of shyness in an earlier chapter about diagnosing your problematic behaviors and mentioned some of the particular problems it causes—mainly, a real difficulty making and sustaining conversation and also difficulty making and sustaining eye contact. Simple shyness is really fixable and a few tricks will allow you to gain confidence for long enough to successfully engage in conversation.

Suggestion for Improvement: Practice Your Social Skills

I suggest that tongue-tied people go out to a social situation or on their date with a list of topics to talk about—topics that are broad enough to discuss without getting into dangerous territory and that will lead to questions that their date, or the person they're getting to know at the bar or at a party, can comfortably answer, too. Talking about your job, sports teams, books, movies, TV shows, current events (though steering clear of hard politics and religion), siblings and any other general subject you can think of are great places to start. Keep the list of topics in your head or written down on a piece of paper in your pocket that you can refer to—in the ladies' or men's room—if you find yourself stuck. Also, before your date, read the paper or watch the news so you can feel well-versed in the world around you. There's nothing worse than someone who's shy and seemingly completely disconnected from normal things such as what movies are playing and who was just elected.

Positive Effect on Intangibles: All those big core issues gathered around self-esteem and self-confidence will benefit greatly from social interaction and conversation becoming easier.

TANGIBLE PROBLEM #5: SOCIAL AWKWARDNESS

We talked about the Awkward Dater and the Shy Dater in that earlier chapter—about how hard it is for people like this to get a date in the first place, let alone make it through that first date and on to a second date. Physical and emotional awkwardness can be huge obstacles to social interaction because not only is the Awkward Dater awkward and uncomfortable, but the person they're trying to talk to ends up feeling awkward and uneasy, too. The Awkward Dater communicates his or her discomfort and before you know it, both people are completely uncomfortable and can't wait for the date or the brief interaction to be over.

Suggestion for Improvement: Therapy or Medication

I believe that most people who come into my office who fall into this category have problems that therapy or medicine can help. When I meet someone who is deeply shy and uncomfortable in their own skin, I almost always tell them that before I can really help them they're going to need to get a different kind of help from a trained professional. The good news is that very often after Awkward Daters do get psychological or medical help, they find they can make changes to their behavior with simple, straightforward behavior-modification techniques that can really improve their social interactions.

Positive Effect on Intangibles: Obviously, working with a good therapist will help you identify and start to cope with your core issues. And the more you work on those core issues, the better and more confident you'll feel about life in general and about the prospect of dating in particular.

TANGIBLE PROBLEM #6: SADNESS OR DEPRESSION

A lot of the people I see who are struggling with issues of sadness or depression do so because of a specific loss, usually the loss of a relationship due to a breakup or a divorce. Some of them are grieving a death: the loss of a parent or close friend or someone else who was important in their life. Sadness and depression can be real obstacles when you're trying to date because those feelings can significantly affect the way you present yourself—how you look, how you dress, the care you take with your hair and makeup, and the topics you focus on in conversation. Often someone who is sad or depressed can come across as too troubled and complicated to take on. Even if the person you're talking to is compassionate and caring and empathetic, your issues could be turnoffs to someone new who is trying to decide if they want to get to know you more.

Suggestion for Improvement: Therapy or Medication

Just as with extremely socially awkward people, those who are sad or depressed almost always need and benefit greatly from therapy, or medication, or both. It might be better to wait until you get help and your mood lifts before you try dating, since your low spirits will likely get in the way of your attempts to connect with new people and will end up only discouraging you. If you struggle less with actual clinical depression and more with general pessimism, it's critical that you start trying to counterbalance every negative thought with a positive one. If you're a pessimist by nature, you're not going to change overnight, but you can start working on seeing your glass as half-full instead of half-empty. Otherwise the negative and dark energy that you carry around with you gets into and affects all of your relationships with friends, family, and coworkers—not just your dating life.

Positive Effect on Intangibles: Working with a good therapist can help you get to the root of your sadness, help you recover from a relationship that ended, and give you constructive assistance in feeling better about yourself and your prospects for future relationships, all of which will improve your self-esteem and renew your hope and faith in yourself as being someone worthy of love. If you're grieving because of a death, joining a bereavement group can give you a place to express your feelings and being among others who are in similar situations will make you feel less alone.

TANGIBLE PROBLEM #7: NEEDINESS, INSECURITY, OR DESPERATION

Nothing's more of a turnoff to both sexes than a needy, insecure, or desperate date, someone who has a palpable sense of neurotic energy and clinginess and gives the unmistakable impression that they have virtually no life and no healthy sense of self outside of the person they used to date or want to date. No one wants a person who is going to place too much importance on you too soon and make you their life preserver. Neediness is a big red flag that a person has issues and problems involving self-esteem and self-image. You don't want to be someone who sends these signals.

Suggestion for Improvement: Get a Life

Not to put too fine a point on it but if you are a needy, insecure, clingy, or desperate person, *get over yourself and get a life.* Reconnect with old friends, connect with new friends, and be engaged in your own life and the activities and interests you used to enjoy. Take an exercise class, or an art class, or do something else you've always wanted to do *but do it by yourself* so that you can make new friends. By taking the pressure off your desperation to find love or to make babies or to not be alone for the rest of your life, you will change the negative, needy energy you've been giving off that has kept people from wanting to connect with you.

Positive Effect on Intangibles: When you get a life and foster your own independence, you will immediately improve your self-esteem and sense of self-worth by relying more on yourself and less on others for the course your life follows. By taking responsibility for your own entertainment and your engagement with the world, you'll automatically gain the empowering feeling that you have control over your life and your own pursuit of happiness. And it's this feeling that will make all the difference in your successful search for love.

TANGIBLE PROBLEM #8: BEING BORING IN BED

This is one of those intangible tangibles—or tangible intangibles— that you may or may not be aware is your problem. Chances are, though, that if you are indeed boring in bed, at some point in your romantic life, someone has told you that, either kindly or unkindly. If your partner was being kind they may have suggested you try to spice things up in the bedroom by trying new things or wearing new things. If they were being unkind, they may have told you to stop lying there like a dead fish. A lack of sexual experience or sexual self-confidence could be at the root of this problem, or you could be inhibited because you don't feel attractive or like the way your body looks. Also, narcissists often have trouble in the bedroom because they think only of their own pleasure and not of their partner's.

Suggestion for Improvement: Improve Your Body Image and Get Comfortable with Your Sexuality

This suggestion is twofold. The first part addresses any insecurities you have about your body: issues you have with your weight or your shape or anything else that makes you feel unattractive and undesirable. Simple diet and exercise is the obvious place to start, but it's not the place to end: you're going to have to feel comfortable with your body at a deeper level. For starters, think about getting a massage or some other kind of body treatment that will make you feel relaxed, and indulge in some nice lingerie and underwear to make you feel sexy. If you're a woman who either hasn't had much sexual experience or despite your experience, has never had an orgasm, it's time that you get in touch with your sexuality—pardon the pun—and figure out how your own body works. If you're not sure whether or not you've had an orgasm, you haven't had one. Buy a vibrator and spend some time getting to know yourself so that when you meet someone special again you'll be able to be more relaxed and expressive with your partner.

Positive Effect on Intangibles: Clearly, when you feel more comfortable with yourself—how you look and how your body works—you're going to start feeling a lot more confident, in and out of the bedroom. Your self-image will improve, your self-esteem will start to soar, and you'll feel an awakening of your libido and a sense that sex is a mutually satisfying experience.

TANGIBLE PROBLEM #9: FINANCIAL TROUBLE

This is a common problem and one that is becoming more and more prevalent in today's tough economy. But the economy has little to do with people who have chronic money problems. Having trouble managing your money can become a huge issue if you don't get help, and it will only lead to more and more stress and misery, which in turn will have an effect on how you feel about yourself and how you approach dating. In fact, if you're someone with chronic financial trouble, problems in your past relationships undoubtedly had something to do with money. Everything is connected in life, and if this is a piece of your puzzle, you have to get over it before you go out there and start looking for love.

Suggestion for Improvement: Get Financial Counseling to Improve Life Skills

Working on this big life skill is easy and straightforward: find a person or a service that will help you with your credit, your finances, and your budget. Whether it's cutting up your credit cards or cutting back on the shopping for a while, you can successfully get a grip on your money problems if you work on it. And there are few things more important to your overall well-being than having a healthy relationship with money and feeling secure in your future.

Positive Effect on Intangibles: Feeling that security in your future and feeling like you can take care of yourself and provide for yourself and that you don't need to depend on others to do those things for you can be enormously satisfying and can really boost your confidence, self-esteem, and sense of accomplishment.

TANGIBLE PROBLEM #10: BEING ANGRY, BITTER, CRITICAL, OR COMPLAINING

Nobody likes mean people, and not only because angry, nasty men and women give off so much negative energy. That sort of nastiness is a red flag for many things: a lack of self-esteem, the absence of happiness, and a profound lack of generosity of spirit. Making fun of people, cutting people down, talking badly of exes or friends, and being overly critical and having no visible empathy, understanding, or kindness toward the people around you is wholly unappealing. What man would want to get involved with a woman so bitchy and caustic that she doesn't have a good word to say about anyone and doesn't seem satisfied by anything? What woman would want to get involved with a man so angry and ugly inside that it would be hard to get through a drinks date with him, let alone contemplate going home with him? If you're angry, bitter, critical, or just plain shitty to the world around you, you'd better get over yourself fast if you ever want to have any chance in hell of finding love and keeping it.

Suggestion for Improvement: Get to the Root of Your Anger

Nothing's going to help you be a nicer person if you don't get to the root of your anger first: the core issue that has made you so mad and so mean for so long. Is it a childhood wound, such as unresolved anger toward a parent or other authority figure? Has feeling wronged by a past spouse or partner left you full of rage and the sense that you've been the victim of some huge injustice? Do you have a general but profound sense of dissatisfaction with how your life has turned out and feel that you've failed more than you've succeeded? Whatever the source of your internal ugliness is, get over it. And get over it fast. Go to therapy, meditate or do yoga, pray or get in touch with your spiritual side—the side of you that connects with something in the universe that's bigger than you and your anger. Believe in something bigger than you and your anger, have faith in something bigger than you and your anger, and in time you will see that anger diminish and your compassion and forgiveness flourish. Go back to the chapter on the mind/body/soul cleanse and spend some time getting to your core, if you haven't done so already, so that this process can begin.

Positive Effect on Intangibles: Anger and ugliness of spirit like this are total deal breakers in relationships—and getting rid of them and resolving your core issues will infuse you with a huge sense of calm and well-being. Make cleansing your anger and starting the process of forgiveness and healing your top priority. Once you've improved significantly you'll be ready to start looking for love.

Now that you're more aware of the ways in which tangible issues can affect other areas in life, use this worksheet to make your own tangibles and intangibles come more into focus.

MAP-OUT-YOUR-OWN-TANGIBLES-AND-INTANGIBLES WORKSHEET

Here are instructions for making your own flow chart that will map out the relationship between your tangibles and intangibles and show how different things will look when you make a change to a tangible.

1. When searching for love, you have to separate the tangibles from the intangibles. Make a list of each.

2. Use the template on the following page to make a flow chart. Insert a primary tangible in the center, and then add above the intangibles that cause it, and below the secondary intangibles that relate to it.

3. Pay special attention to the flow chart box or boxes above the primary tangible you're mapping: that is, the major intangibles that are your core issues.

4. Don't beat yourself up about either your intangibles or your tangibles. Remember to treat yourself with the kindness and compassion we discussed throughout the "Getting to Your Core" section and specifically in the "Facing Your Demons" chapter. Now's the perfect time to put some of those abstract principles into practice.

5. Come up with a plan for working on one of your tangibles. If it's related to weight or fitness, make an easy diet and exercise plan you can stick to and one that you will have quick success with. When you eliminate or improve on a tangible—even just slightly—your attitude will automatically start to improve, which will in turn lead to changes in your intangibles.

6. Look at your flow chart again. This time, change your primary tangible so that it reflects the change you plan on making. For instance, if you had "weight" as your primary tangible, change it to "weight loss" or "healthy lifestyle." Then look at the connected boxes and think about how those related tangibles would be affected. Make changes to those boxes, too.

7. Now consider all the changes you've made to your chart and think about how these changes would positively affect your intangibles. Make changes, however slight, to those boxes, too. For instance, if "low self-esteem" is an intangible related to your "weight" tangible, write "improved self-esteem" to show how your future weight loss would affect that issue.

DO-IT-YOURSELF MAP-OUT-YOUR-OWN-TANGIBLES-AND-INTANGIBLES WORKSHEET

FIG. 3. RELATIONSHIP OF TANGIBLES AND INTANGIBLES BEFORE CHANGES

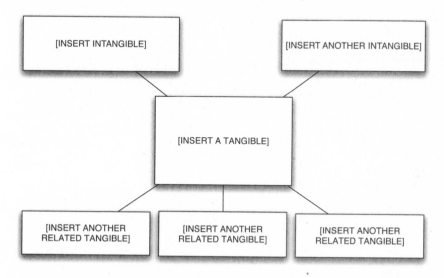

FIG. 4. RELATIONSHIP OF TANGIBLES AND INTANGIBLES AFTER CHANGES

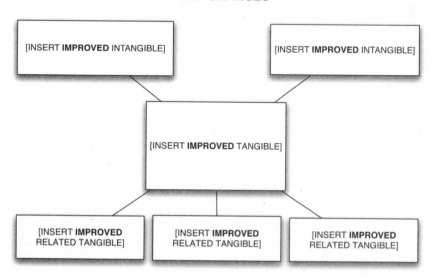

9

Attitude Adjustment

A Crash Course in Getting Over Yourself

It's time now to really get to the nitty-gritty—and that means putting the finishing touches on the attitudes and behaviors and skills that will make all the difference in whether you succeed or fail when you go out there and start dating.

In some ways dating is like looking for a job: you have to make sure you're ready to hit the pavement and sell yourself. When you're job hunting, you need to look your best, feel your best, and act your best so that the person who's in a position to hire you for a particular job will see that you're the perfect applicant. You spend hours writing a résumé that highlights your skills and goals, picking out proper business attire that fits well and makes you look polished and professional, psyching yourself up mentally and emotionally to put your best self forward, and making sure your self-esteem and your communication skills are at their absolute best. Think of this final stretch of preparation as you would the preparation for that job search: We're going to make sure you're completely ready to face the dating world and that you're at your best when you start meeting people and start looking to find love.

Get out your notebooks and put your thinking caps back on because the work we're going to do in this chapter is all in your head!

GET OVER YOUR NEGATIVITY!

One of the biggest obstacles my clients have to overcome isn't physical. It isn't their weight or their hair or the aesthetics of their smile. It isn't how much money they earn, or what they do for a living, or how much education they have.

It's their attitude.

Their negative attitude, to be more exact.

Positive thinking and a positive attitude lead to positive happenings, but you'd be surprised by how few people who walk into my office put that concept into practice.

Sometimes a client with a big attitude problem will come in. They're testy or angry or rude or just not very nice, and I won't be able to help myself. I'll say to them, "Well no wonder you're single! You're a bitch!"

Which is my way of saying: *Get over yourself and your negativity unless you want to spend the rest of your life alone!*

Positive daters, even if they're average looking—which most of the time they are—have a much better chance of being successful than negative daters because they're willing to try new things and are flexible in what types of people they're willing to meet.

Positive daters are positive about life in general and not just about dating. They have a healthy sense of self and self-esteem, and they're not carrying around a heavy burden of unresolved anger or sadness. Whether they've made peace with their pasts and healed their wounds long ago or just recently, they're grounded in the present and excited about their future—a future filled with the possibility of finding love.

Open-mindedness, flexibility, and—never forget this one—a sense of humor are the hallmarks of the positive dater, and it's those qualities you have to adopt if you want to succeed at dating and love.

GET OVER YOUR FANTASY OF PERFECTION!

This, believe it or not, is one of the most important messages in the book: *the world is full of average and being average is okay!*

Think about it for a minute: how strange it sounds to be told to accept your averageness and make peace with the idea that you're not the most fabulous person on the planet. To be told that you're probably never going to win a beauty pageant or a nationally televised reality talent show or come up with the next billion-dollar business.

It goes against almost everything we're taught as children—especially in America, the land of dreamers and thinking big and limitless opportunity and possibility—and against almost everything we see in magazines and on television and at the movies. Because our culture has become increasingly obsessed with perfection—namely physical perfection—and with celebrity many people get confused between fantasy and reality.

People, the reality is this: Most of you reading this book right now are average looking. If someone had a clipboard out right now and was rating you, you'd fall solidly in the middle and normal range of attractiveness and you'd fall solidly in the middle and normal range of intelligence, career success, yearly salary, and all that other stuff we've come to measure ourselves and one another by.

And most of the people you're going to date are average looking and of average intelligence and have achieved an average level of career and financial success.

The world is full of average.

And average is okay!

If you're looking for perfection—in yourself and others—*get over yourself!*

In terms of dating, it's crucial that you understand and accept and internalize this message. If you don't, you're never going to be able to accept your flaws and imperfections, and even more important, you're never going to be able to accept the flaws and imperfections in others. And believe me when I say that if you can't accept the fact that people aren't perfect, you're not going to have much luck finding love.

Of course, to accept—and embrace—your averageness doesn't

mean that you can't and shouldn't strive to improve yourself in all ways. But those improvements and refinements should be seen for what they are: gravy on top of the good and special person that you already are.

Accepting your averageness and the averageness of others isn't about settling for someone you're not interested in or not attracted to. It isn't about giving up your hopes and dreams for great chemistry and a deep connection with another person. It's about living firmly in reality instead of in fantasy. Once you accept the fact that you're never going to date Brad Pitt and that you're never going to look like Angelina Jolie—no matter how many men you date and how many matchmakers you go to—you'll be able to see your date for who he is: someone who might just be a wonderful and warm and caring guy who thinks you're the most amazing woman he's ever met.

And isn't that what falling in love is all about? Realizing that the person you've gotten to know and who has gotten to know you—that average human person with all their human flaws and imperfections—is the most amazing person on the planet?

GET OVER YOUR UGLY!

This is one of those childhood issues with very deep roots, and it's something that can really mess you up in adulthood if you don't work hard at getting over it. Walking around feeling like the ugly little girl or ugly little boy you once were—or thought you were— has a huge effect on your dating life and is probably one reason people who haven't gotten over their ugly have big problems finding and keeping love.

This is why:

If you're someone who was unattractive as a child or thought you were unattractive as a child—and I was one of those people, by the way, with my chubbiness and my glasses and my seizures—and you don't get over it, you're going to carry it around with you and spend your life reacting to all the pain it caused you.

No matter how much better you look now, you're always going to see the person you used to see in the mirror—the fat person or the kid with big glasses and braces, or some other vision of unattractiveness.

And no matter how many times people try to tell you that you're not ugly—that you're pretty or handsome or sexy or terrific looking—it won't help. Because the voice inside your head is still telling you the opposite.

Men who were late bloomers—who used to be big geeks or nerds when they were young and who eventually grew into their bodies and their personalities—sometimes become commitment-phobic Party Boys who now need the constant attention of very attractive women to make them feel attractive. In other words, to compensate for their difficult time with girls as adolescents, they want to become the arm candy of beautiful women who make them feel less ugly as an adult.

Women who were late bloomers—who used to be heavy or who never felt beautiful—sometimes become Shallow Daters for much the same reason: they need to be with men who are 8s and 9s so that they can convince the world, and themselves, that they can attract handsome men.

In order to have healthy relationships in the future and to feel good about yourself, which will in turn help you attract good people, you have to get over yourself.

You have to get over your ugly.

You have to find your own inner beauty before you can ever hope to find love.

STOP THE BOOTY CALLS!

I've been thinking a lot about the issue of the booty call lately because I recently met a woman who is a divorce attorney. Our conversations—the divorce lawyer meets the matchmaker—have been interesting because we've had a lot to talk about given our opposite sides of the fence: she gets women before the booty calls, when they're excited about acting out their new sense of freedom after a bad marriage. And I get them afterward—after their booty calls have left them feeling lonely and alone, more lonely and alone than they felt even during the worst times in their marriages.

You gals out there who still think that booty calls are a sign of feminism: they're more like the booby prize of feminism.

Because booty calls aren't a positive way to embrace your sexuality.

They're a negative expression of your low self-esteem.

I speak as a professional—as someone who is part matchmaker and part dating coach. And I speak from personal experience—from when I was single for a short time after my divorce.

Booty calls undermine romance because there are no rules, no obligations, no meaningful attachments between you and the person you're hooking up with for the night. Why bother going to a nice restaurant if you're just going to end up in the bedroom? Why bother seeing a movie together or going to a club to listen to some music when the whole point is quick sex?

When women ask me how they can turn a booty call into a romantic relationship, I tell them they can't because it's probably too late. If their "relationship" started in the bedroom it's likely it will end there, too. If the message you're giving with your behavior is that all you want is a one night stand and cheap sex, that's all you'll get.

At worst, booty calls can be dangerous, and at best, they are cheap sex, and cheap sex isn't good sex—especially for women, who often need to be emotionally involved to reach their sexual potential. Ironically, a lot of the women having booty calls are trying to find what they only have in their dreams and in their fantasies: great hot sex. Orgasms. But it's misguided to think that they'll eventually have an orgasm if they just keep trying with different men.

Some of you might disagree with me. You might be thinking that booty calls are fun, and that you don't feel bad about them or about yourself the next morning, or even that the sex is great.

To which I say, *Get over yourself!*

Women who have lots of booty calls are looking for something from sex. Maybe their libido has skyrocketed after a divorce or breakup, or they're looking for validation after a loveless or sexless marriage or relationship.

But if you're looking for love you have to say no to the booty call.

If you want the real thing, stop doing the fake thing.

And if you want to feel good about yourself, stop doing something that makes you feel so bad the next day.

Saying no to the booty call isn't about being submissive or giving up the ground we've gained through feminism. Saying no to the booty call is the ultimate way you can show yourself and the men you're looking to date that you have self-respect.

And that you're serious about finding love.

And that you're ready to find love.

HAND OVER THE PICKLE JAR!

What has happened to the intestinal fortitude of men? Why is it that so many of the men I see in my matchmaking life don't have—if you'll pardon the expression—balls?

It's my opinion that men are the most indecisive creatures on the planet, although when they finally make a decision they never look back. It's also my opinion that with the growing independence of women comes the struggle of men to feel like men. And the reason for this is that as women have been forced into independence they've forgotten that they still have to allow men to feel needed.

I know when I talk about this topic it makes a lot of women uncomfortable because it sounds politically incorrect and it also sounds like I'm telling women not to be strong and capable and successful.

That's not what I'm saying at all.

What I am saying, though, is that if you express to a man all the masculine traits you've acquired in your singleness—especially if you express it during the first three dates—you will probably be alone for the rest of your life!

Why?

I don't know why men still can't handle the extreme independence of women, but they can't, so just stop bragging about how important you are at work and how great you are at fixing your car and painting your house and traveling the world by yourself—and how fine you are without a man and how much you don't need one.

In other words, *Get over yourself and hand over the pickle jar!*

That is, even though you're strong and independent and capable and can open your own pickle jar, if you're with a guy and you have a pickle jar that needs opening, let him open it!

Anyone who knows me knows that I'm 100 percent in support

of women and a feminist to my core. I've worked all my life, been a single mother for the last decade, and started a successful match-making business. Anyone who knows me also knows that I'm not a pushover and not someone who believes in anything that would truly compromise the authenticity of the soul by telling you to pre-tend to be something you're really not.

But ladies, please: letting a guy open a pickle jar even though you could open it yourself isn't something that will truly compromise the authenticity of your soul.

It's not about pretending that you can't open it.

It's about choosing to let him open it so that he can feel needed. Because men need to feel needed.

Sometimes the Pickle Jar Effect can be seen when there's no pickle jar involved. For example, one client I had, Katie, could never seem to get past the first date. After I'd observed her behavior and her dating skills in action, I realized that her problem was her take-charge one-upping attitude. She always had to show the man she was on a date with that she was right and that she knew more than he did about anything and everything.

On one date, she corrected her date's pronunciation of a French dish he was ordering, adding that she spoke fluent French because she'd lived in France. When he commented that he'd lived in France, too, the summer after college, she one-upped him by saying she'd lived there for a whole year during college. While making plans for another date with another man, she overruled two of his restaurant suggestions until he suggested that she should decide where they were going since it clearly mattered more to her than it did to him.

That kind of bossy and one-upping attitude isn't attractive in anyone—male or female—but it can be a bigger turnoff to men. Sometimes what happens when we spend so much time alone and on our own is that we forget to let them open the stupid pickle jar. We forget to let them make some decisions, take charge, and feel strong.

Remember, I don't make the rules, I just follow them. And one thing I don't think will ever change is that a man still needs to feel like a man and be needed. So if you're alone and you need a jar opened, go ahead and open your own pickle jar.

But if he's around, hand it over and let him do it. It's just as easy to ask him to open it and know that you are the smarter, clever one for doing it.

It's about attitude.

LISTENING TO UNDERSTAND

Really listening to someone in order to understand them—what I call "empathic listening"—is one of the most important life skills you can develop. And in terms of dating skills, it's at the top of the list of key components for becoming a successful dater and finding love.

Empathic listening is what I do every day, with every client. In fact, it's what I do all the time, whenever I'm communicating with someone, whether I'm talking to a client, a friend, my daughter, or someone I've just met. Asking questions and actually listening to the answers a person gives you is a skill that most people fail to develop, and it's one of the reasons why human connection has become so difficult. We're so busy and self-absorbed that we often don't take the time and make the effort to listen to another person's story and truly hear and feel what they're saying.

I believe that we all have the capacity for this kind of communication—and that to improve this underdeveloped skill takes awareness and practice.

This is one of the most vital dating skills you can have. Put another way: without the ability to listen to understand, you're going to be single for a very long time.

When you're sitting across from someone, talking on a first date, trying to find common ground, trying to decide if there's chemistry or even just the possibility of chemistry, trying to process a whole lot of information—what they're wearing and saying and doing— it's easy to forget to listen. To listen and really hear who they are and what they're about.

Listening and hearing, of course, are important on a very basic level. Often if you really listen to what someone tells you about who they are and what they're like, and if you really hear what they're telling you, you might process certain facts and decide you don't want to date them—and spare yourself a lot of unhappiness down the road. People drop a lot of bread crumbs along the way in con-

versation—clues to who they really are—and if you're paying attention you'll be able to disqualify the narcissists and commitment-
phobes early on.

But the main reason empathic listening is included in this chapter is that if you truly want to connect with someone—at a party, on
a date, sitting across the table from you—you need to learn how to
listen.

So that you'll be able to respond.

There are some people—men and women—for whom attractiveness is not the problem. They don't have any trouble attracting
dates or lovers. But they do have trouble keeping those dates or
lovers interested, because their ego or their sense of grandiosity or
plain old self-centeredness gets in the way of truly connecting.

One client I had recently fits this category to a tee. Now in her
late twenties, Stephanie was always attractive and had always used
her beauty to get through life. Well-educated and moving up the
corporate ladder in her career in sales, Stephanie had developed a
big ego and a certain grandiosity—traits that didn't serve her well in
her work life or her dating life, both of which required her to connect with people on a deeper level than she was capable of. While
her physical appeal lured the men she dated and the clients she sold
to, her shallowness and lack of emotional connection eventually
turned them off.

Because despite her physical appeal and initial charm, Stephanie
was too selfish to understand and mirror the people she was dealing
with.

"Mirroring"—a sales term, in fact—is when you take into account the person you're talking to and adjust your behavior or your
conversation accordingly. That means clueing in to and being sensitive to topics that the other person might not be entirely comfortable discussing (education level or career trajectory, to name only
two) or to attitudes that don't mesh with theirs. In Stephanie's work
life, she often hit a brick wall with her small-town clients and
couldn't close deals with them because she had trouble understanding that her constant bragging about her big job and fancy down-
town loft was off-putting. Not only did it make her buyers feel
inferior and insecure about their lack of sophistication or knowledge of the movies and stores and clothing brands she often refer-

enced in conversation, but it made them feel that she didn't "get" them and that she didn't really care.

Stephanie blamed others for her failures at work and problems with relationships. It was always someone else's fault, in her opinion. But it was clear to me that Stephanie's biggest problem was her lack of communication skills—namely, her inability to listen and mirror. I told her that her ego was getting in the way, and until she stopped talking about herself and being so self-absorbed and she started asking questions and making eye contact—until she got over herself—she was never going to have success at work or in love.

STOP BLAMING ONE SINGLE THING FOR WHY YOU'RE SINGLE

I recently had a female client named Val, who was thirty-six years old, a little chunky but very attractive and likeable, and earning a great living. Within the first fifteen minutes of the interview she told me that her life sucked and that the reason it sucked and the reason she was still single was because of one thing and one thing only:

The fact that she didn't sing anymore.

At first I thought she meant singing at home—in the shower, or in the car, or in the rain—as if singing were a metaphor for vitality and hope and expressing happiness. What she meant was singing professionally, giving classical voice lessons, and doing vocals for some moderately successful local bands.

I thought Val was cute and smart despite the fact that it seemed ridiculous that she was blaming everything that was wrong in her life on one single thing.

"You're out of balance," I told her. "You need a chiropractor for your head!"

I knew that Val was like many frustrated singles who want to point the finger at one single factor that can explain their problematic or nonexistent love life, and I knew that not singing professionally was not Val's problem. At least, not in the way she thought it was.

Val thought the fact that she wasn't singing anymore was the reason her life was a mess. She hated her new job and felt she wasn't being true to herself as an artist and a performer. But Val's problem was that she was stuck in the past. She was still upset about having to give up singing because she couldn't earn enough of a living from it and she was still angry that she had to give up her dream job for a boring job-job.

I had a feeling that one reason this had affected her dating life was that she kept telling her dates about it: how she used to sing professionally and how life sucked now that she'd stopped. I also suspected that her disappointment and discontent were making her feel shitty enough about herself to score booty calls, and I was right. And living in the past and scoring booty calls are two things that won't get you anywhere in your search for love.

Val had a good sense of humor about herself. When I told her that blaming everything on her not singing was ridiculous, she agreed, and after we had a good laugh about it, she said she wanted to dig in and start cleaning up her act.

And so we focused on her biggest tangible—her dissatisfaction about not singing.

I explained to her that singing was something she enjoyed and it was an art form she loved, but that it wasn't who she was. It was something she loved to do, but in the end she couldn't make a living doing it.

Work, I told her, is a means to live, and having a passion for your work—like my passion for matchmaking—can make you good at it. But work doesn't make you who you are, either. You're still you when you leave work at the end of the day, no matter what you do. Even if your job isn't the most fulfilling, it doesn't mean that you have to feel unfulfilled about everything.

Making that distinction—understanding the separation between self and work, career and identity—helped Val to see that whether she sang professionally had nothing to do with her problems with dating. Her real problem was the attitude that had her looking for something to blame, living in the past, feeling like a failed artist. She realized she would have to get over herself in order to reenter and fully engage in her present.

Sometimes you have to adjust your attitude. You have to learn to be more positive than negative about life and dating or learn to be more realistic and accepting of yourself and others for not being perfect 10s, or learn to value yourself and like yourself enough to get over feeling ugly and to stop the booty calls, or to understand how important it is to make the person you date feel needed and wanted even if you're the most independent woman in the world. These are crucial points to fine-tune before you take your final steps toward finding love.

Internet Dating

Why Online Dating Should Be a Means to an End Instead of the End Itself and How It Can Help You Practice Your Dating Skills

Lots of people ask me about Internet dating: what I think about it, whether it works, if it's safe. And when they ask I usually tell them how I feel.

I don't love Internet dating, and not because I think it's competition for the service I try to provide my clients; there's really no comparison between the two. But I think that Internet dating doesn't begin to even approximate the process of in-person dates found the old-fashioned way, and I also think it's too easy for people to be dishonest about themselves online, which makes your screening process even harder than it already is.

But I also know that Internet dating isn't going anywhere. Sixteen million people visited Internet dating sites in 2006, according to the Pew Internet and American Life Project's online dating survey. So instead of just complaining about it and telling you all the things that are wrong with it, I'm going to talk about what you can do to be safe—physically and emotionally—if you choose to use it and how you can increase your chances for success.

The first and most important thing I tell clients is: don't go into it thinking you're going to meet the love of your life. You might. But you probably won't. Instead, I tell them to think of online dating as a networking tool that can help them become more social.

Internet dating has some positives. The main one is that it can be especially good for people who haven't had much experience with dating, such as shy and socially awkward daters, or people who haven't been part of the singles scene for a long time and are completely out of practice, like the recently divorced or widowed. But even to the basic average normal dater, computer dating sites provide the opportunity to meet someone new and, at the very least, perhaps make a new friend.

Probably, though, if you're reading this book, you're not here just to make new friends.

You probably have enough friends.

Many of whom are single, just like you.

No, if you're reading this book you want more than friendship—you want to connect with someone on a meaningful level and you want to feel chemistry.

Which is why Internet dating—in moderation—is sometimes better than no dating at all.

INTERNET DATING: POSITIVES

There are a few benefits of Internet dating—again, in moderation:

- It can help you identify your dating weaknesses and strengths.
- It can help you develop and improve your dating skills.
- It can give you the opportunity to have "practice dates."
- It can increase your dating pool geographically.
- Targeted specialty sites can provide access to religious, ethnic, racial, and social groups you have things in common with and want to connect to.

But despite these positives it's very important to understand this: many people go online to play, and some people who go online to play are married or otherwise unavailable.

And: it's easy to get addicted to living in a fantasy world and acting like someone you're not.

So, buyer beware.

INTERNET DATING: NEGATIVES

The main reason I'm not a big fan of the Internet when it comes to dating is that it isn't possible to use the normal screening process that I use when I meet clients and make matches and that you use when meeting someone for the first time: seeing someone in person and actually talking to them. When you take away the in-person meeting, you eliminate all the important tools humans use to judge others and process who they are: what they look like, what they're wearing, how they talk, and how they present themselves to us and to the world.

Thousands of tiny pieces of crucial information are revealed when we meet someone. Taken together as a whole, these pieces of information are clues to a person's personality, character, and emotional life. What they're wearing and how they're groomed—clothes and shoes and accessories and hair and makeup—not only shows their sense of style (or lack of it), but also gives you a window into their level of self-esteem. Does the person take pride in their appearance? Do they make an effort to look good—or at least presentable? Do they seem comfortable in their own skin and in their body, whatever their size or shape?

How many times have you gone out on a date with someone and immediately noticed something that, from the get-go, bothered you?

Maybe the guy was wearing too much aftershave or cologne.

Or he wasn't wearing enough deodorant.

Or his nails were bitten down to the nubs.

Maybe the woman was wearing too much makeup.

Or no makeup at all.

Or her hair was really big.

Fair or not, those are all things that go into the pot when we're evaluating someone and their potential compatibility with us.

Sometimes it's not about looks. It's about some other quality that is uniquely theirs. They might have a really loud voice, or a really annoying laugh, or they might mumble when they talk. Maybe they don't make that important eye contact that we've already talked about, or maybe they stare at you too much or make you uncomfortable for reasons that you just can't explain. These are things that reveal themselves when people get together, face-to-face, and start the process of getting to know each other.

But when you meet someone online, this doesn't happen.

Instead, you sit at your computer and click on people's profiles. You look at their photos, which could be ten or twenty years old. And you read their self-descriptions, which could be a little bit exaggerated . . . or hugely exaggerated. And you either like what you see or you don't, even though you're basing that opinion on a very small amount of information that isn't even necessarily trustworthy. When you're assessing someone only from a one-dimensional online profile, you have such limited information that you'll be making a snap judgment you might not have made in person. Sure, you might have come to a similar conclusion had you met the prospective date in person, but more often than not, people dismiss potential dates online whom they might have given a second look in person.

DISHONESTY AND MISREPRESENTATION ARE RAMPANT ON THE INTERNET

We all tell white lies on occasion, and we all inadvertently (or purposefully) manipulate others to aid our own agendas. The opportunities for people to be untruthful are common enough in real life, but in a virtual reality—which is to say, a kind of nonreality reality—the potential for dishonesty is even higher. All you have is someone's words on the screen to go by, and some people, when given the chance, will lie if they think it'll improve their odds in the dating scene. At the very least, you could be dealing with an inflated online profile or an out-of-date twenty-pounds-lighter picture. At its worst, Internet dating deception can take other more serious forms of misrepresentation.

All that potential for dishonesty puts an extra burden on the screening process, which can be very overwhelming as you try to figure out what's fact and what's fiction, separate lies from the truth. You now have to become a detective, someone who looks at the information in an online profile with a skeptical and distrustful eye, and being skeptical and distrustful isn't the best way to start your search for true love.

If a man is 5'7" and posting his profile on a dating site, he's probably not going to tell just a white lie and say he's 5'8". He's going to say he's 5'10". Or "almost six feet."

If he's bald he's probably going to post a photo from when he still had hair.

If a woman is forty she's probably going to say she's thirty-five.

And if she weighs 160 pounds she's probably going to say she's 140 pounds.

Or 135 pounds.

Or leave the line blank altogether.

Or post a five-year-old photo taken when she was thirty-five years old and 135 pounds.

You have to be wary, leary, and suspicious as you browse profiles, and most people don't like having to think that way.

SPENDING TOO MUCH TIME ON INTERNET DATING SITES = ONLINE CHEMISTRY AND FANTASY RELATIONSHIPS

We all want to fall in love and be romantic, for sure, but most of the time people who fall in love online are falling in love with a fantasy—the fantasy the other person has created in the form of a profile and persona in order to attract online attention.

And the fantasy of online chemistry. Which is one of the biggest emotional risks of Internet dating.

Dating is about chemistry and we build chemistry in person.

And while we sometimes build it on the Internet, or on the phone, or through text messages, the totality of people's chemistry isn't there.

We process emotional and physical cues in real time, in real life, and generally we come to our conclusions, right or wrong, pretty quickly. It takes ten seconds to pass or fail the physical chemistry test and thirty minutes to pass or fail the emotional chemistry test. Not a lot of time either way to make a good impression, but with online dating this natural and most basic part of the screening process—otherwise known as the first impression—doesn't exist.

Using the Internet too much has side effects, like too much of anything does. Some of the risks and downsides of being addicted to your computer for socializing are obvious and some aren't, but it's important to be aware of all of them.

- Getting involved and emotionally intimate with a complete stranger who's a veteran at trolling the Internet puts you at risk for stalking, date rape, and other kinds of physical harm and financial fraud
- Relying too much on a virtual world instead of participating in the real world
- Using your computer as a way of avoiding actual dating
- Creating online chemistry with people you don't even know
- Creating dangerous and fictional relationships through your computer
- Setting yourself up for major disappointment when these "relationships" don't work out or when you discover that the person you were having this "relationship" with doesn't really exist
- Getting addicted to the voyeuristic aspect of socializing on the Internet

INTERNET DATING ADDICTION

As a matchmaker, I'm always trying to figure people out and get to the bottom of why they do what they do. And in my opinion, the root of spending too much time on Internet dating sites is voyeuristic.

Voyeurism, basically defined, is deriving sexual pleasure from observing other people. Men who regularly go to strip clubs and use porn are obviously engaging in voyeurism. Most of them know that what they're seeing isn't real but what habitual users of porn may not know is why they're drawn to it: because they're more comfortable in a fantasy world than they are in the real world.

In other words, they're afraid of the real thing.

In much the same way, people whose primary source of social interaction is their computer—people who prefer to interact intimately with people in a virtual world instead of in the real world—

almost always have a fear of intimacy. They feel safest socializing from a distance, watching others interact, or engaging in online relationships that never leave cyberspace, with their true identities always cloaked in anonymity.

Whenever clients tell me stories about online relationships with men and women all over the country, far from where they themselves live, I have to remind them that these relationships aren't real. Even if the feelings are.

I remind them that their fear of intimacy or their avoidance of the dating scene has gotten to a point where they're replacing human intimacy with instant messaging.

I remind them that otherwise normal, healthy people who are lonely can go astray on the Internet.

And I remind them that even though they think Internet dating is better than nothing, sometimes if it's all you do—if it's the only thing you do—it *isn't* better.

In order to find love—real love with a real person—you're going to have to step away from the computer and go out there and meet people.

And nothing can ever replace real human contact.

HONESTY IS THE BEST POLICY

If you choose to try out Internet dating, there is one ground rule that I hope you'll follow: be honest when writing your online profile. Most people assume that because they're being honest when they write their profiles, everyone else is being honest when they write theirs.

Not exactly.

But that doesn't mean you should pad your online résumé to the point where it backfires: after all, if you plan on someday meeting the person you're getting to know online and you lie about your weight, they're going to notice that you're 200 pounds and not 150.

So women: stop lying about your weight.

And men: stop lying about your height.

Lying puts you in a position to be rejected—sooner, or later. And I don't care if you meet someone in a bar, through a matchmaker, or online: people can sense when you're being fake.

PATTI'S BASIC RULES FOR ONLINE DATING

- Make online dating your practice, not your process. Use your dates with the people you meet through Internet dating sites to get back in the swing of dating if you haven't dated in a while or as a way to practice your dating skills. Pay attention on those dates to your weak skills (not putting enough time or effort into your pre-date appearance, or sending the wrong message to dates because you're too provocatively dressed) and your strengths (making conversation and listening) so that you know what you need to work on when you really start dating.
- Sign up for only one month at a time with a maximum of six months. Any longer than that will turn the benefits of Internet dating into a crutch and become an obstacle to real-life dating.
- Look at each month of Internet dating as a short-term thirty-day goal to work on the dating objectives you've set for yourself.
- Send no more than three emails to an online prospect. If you have more to say, do it in person (see below).
- Correspond for no more than thirty days with an online prospect. After thirty days, you should meet already!
- Allow yourself minimal contact through instant messaging (IMing).
- Don't use your full name or provide any personal information including phone number, home address, or work address, and don't reveal any information about your children including their names or ages.
- Except for possibly using a different name if it makes you feel more comfortable, be truthful in your profile.
- Understand that using a sexy or suggestive user name might attract attention from people you don't actually want to date.
- Keep a dating journal: write down the names of your dates and any visual details that will help you remember who they are. Also make notes about personality traits, interests, and any other thoughts you had while interacting with them in person.

Part of the process of getting over yourself and getting ready to find love is being honest with yourself and with others, which means it's important to be aboveboard in your profile, both in describing yourself and in describing what you're looking for. If you don't want to date someone who is overweight, then say so. It doesn't do you any good to have a lot of dates with people who aren't what you're looking for. And it doesn't do the people you meet any good if your profile says you don't care about weight or height or religious preference when you actually do care: you're only going to hurt them when you reject them down the road, and you'll only be hurt when someone rejects you down the road because you weren't what you advertised.

Honesty, of course, has its limits. Some people think that they have to be brutally honest about themselves to the point that the way they describe themselves is a huge turnoff. Don't forget that the point here is to sell yourself, so you should describe yourself and your traits in the best possible terms. Instead of describing yourself as "argumentative," use the word "opinionated." Instead of saying you're "controlling," say you're "highly organized."

Learning how to describe yourself accurately and positively is an important part of the dating process, and this is the perfect place to start.

TAKING ONLINE DATING OFF-LINE

At a certain point, after all the browsing and profile-reading and emailing and chatting, it's time to take the next step: meeting the person you've been corresponding with online.

This is one of the most critical parts of the process of computer dating because this is the point at which you stop living in a virtual world and step back into the real one: the world of where to meet and what to wear and what to say. Sometimes people spend so much time at their computer screens and keyboards that they forget dating means you have to actually get dressed and leave your house.

But meeting the person you've met online is also the most risky part of the process, and not just because of issues of physical safety. It's challenging because it's the point at which your fantasy relationship meets reality: the person you've had chemistry with over the computer, this person who's been writing flirtatious emails and sending suggestive instant messages and whose profile promises a Johnny Depp look-alike or Jennifer Aniston clone might just turn out to be nothing like their online persona.

In other words, they might turn out to be average.

Or worse, way below average.

Which is highly likely since most real people won't live up to the fantasy the two of you have spent hours creating.

In order to reduce your avoidance of real-life dating and minimize the risk of setting yourself up for disappointment by creating online chemistry with someone you've never met in person, make your transition from online dating to off-line dating physically and emotionally safer and potentially more successful by following my rules and advice:

- After three emails or thirty days, suggest a meeting. If your online prospect declines but continues to want to correspond through email, you know that this person only wants a virtual connection.
- Pick a busy and very public place for your first meeting: a popular restaurant with a foyer. Again, don't use your last name or give your home phone number to your date or to the restaurant.
- Meet at the restaurant. Do not have your date pick you up or take you home.
- Let a friend or coworker know you're getting together with someone you've met online, and make sure you're specific about where you're meeting and when you're meeting.
- Before the date, arrange to have a friend call you about twenty minutes into the date to check in with you and make sure you're okay.
- Like any other first date, keep it short (sixty to ninety minutes) and simple (don't expect to wine and dine).
- Don't get drunk: too much alcohol will affect your judgment and put you at risk for potentially dangerous and unsafe situations.
- Focus on the here-and-now, and don't discuss previous experiences with disastrous relationships.
- Approach each date with a lighthearted, nondesperate attitude. While you're trying to find true love, accept the fact that the dating process takes time and that it's a numbers game: the

more people you meet, the more chances you have for meeting someone special.

TAKE THE RUDENESS AND INSINCERITY OUT OF INTERNET DATING

Sometimes we are so concerned with our own issues—our insecurities about our looks or our prospects for finding a good relationship, our fear of being disappointed or hurt in the process of looking for love—that we forget the other person has their own issues. Not to mention, feelings.

One of the problems with computer dating is that on a very basic level it dehumanizes the process of dating and personal interaction. Because of the buttons and the keys and the screens and the instant messages, we forget that we're communicating with an actual person.

Most of my clients who have used computer dating services end up frustrated, angry, and exhausted because most of their experiences weren't good ones: they encountered people who lied or misrepresented themselves, and they were disappointed when the chemistry they'd created online didn't spark with the person they are finally sitting across from.

But rudeness and insensitivity—that hurt-or-be-hurt mentality—only makes things worse. Part of the journey of getting over yourself so that you can be ready to find true love includes adopting an attitude of kindness and a spirit of generosity toward others. The only time that this doesn't apply is when you're dealing with an Internet liar, because they're not entitled to your generosity and kindness if they've misled you or misrepresented themselves.

Part Four

over it

11

First Date 101

It Is What It Is, But It Isn't Rocket Science

Learning how to succeed on a first date shouldn't be that hard. In reality, succeeding on a first date *isn't* that hard. The key is to follow some simple rules about what to do and what not to do. One of these guidelines is to accept that one reason you've had trouble with dating in the past is because of something *you've* been doing or not doing.

This isn't about blaming you for your dating problems. It is about making you see that dating isn't some mysterious, incomprehensible process you have no control over. There are parts of the dating process that you can control—such as improving your dating skills—which can make all the difference between a bad first date and a great first date.

In the previous sections of this book, we spent a lot of time digging around in your core to get at the big issues contributing to your dating problems, and healing the wounds of your past so you could move on to your future.

Well, giddyup, people, because your future is here now, and it's time to get you to the end of this book and off the couch and out to where you can find true love.

To simplify and demystify things, let's go over the main objectives of the First Date:

- To have fun and make a new friend
- To get through it without turning someone off completely
- To determine if there's any chemistry—physical or emotional
- To figure out whether or not you want to see the person again

As you can see, the goals are fairly limited and relatively modest: which is to say, it shouldn't be too hard to be able to get to the end of a first date having accomplished all of them.

But why is it that some people can't make it through a first date without accomplishing *any* of those objectives?

Why is it that otherwise intelligent and successful people— clients I see and people reading this book—find it almost impossible to get through the basics of a first date with barely a passing grade?

One reason why people have such a hard time with first dates is that they can't handle the pressure of performance: Their insecurity or shyness or lack of dating experience or bad self-image causes them to feel nervous.

And when you're nervous, you're not yourself.

And there's never a time when it's more important to be yourself than on a first date.

Another reason why people have such a hard time with first dates is they think that "being yourself" means showing up to a first date looking exactly like you look at home and behaving exactly the way you do with your family and friends.

I like my look, clients will tell me when I scold them for having shown up to a date wearing sweatpants and a wrinkled shirt, or when they've told their entire life story to someone they barely know. *This is who I am.*

To which I say, *Get over yourself!*

I'm not going to guarantee that you'll find the person of your dreams the minute you put this book down if you follow these guidelines, but I truly believe that you'll have a better chance of connecting with someone really great than you would if you kept doing things the way you've been doing them.

Before moving on, though, it's worth looking at the big picture to understand the larger goal of the first date:

Getting a second date.

And getting to a second date—or a third or a fourth or a fifth—requires that you have a clear understanding and working knowledge of what makes a love relationship healthy and strong and successful.

In my experience, both professional and personal, as a matchmaker and as a person who's lived life and made mistakes along the way, these are the three most important things in a relationship:

- Respect
- Sense of humor
- Sex

In that order.

You may disagree, or you might put them in a different order, but whatever way you want to break things down, these are the crucial fundamentals of any love relationship.

Without respect—mutual respect—the fun you have together and the chemistry you feel with each other won't matter.

Without a sense of humor, the difficulties and complexities of your life as a couple and your lives as individuals will overwhelm you.

And without good sex—without compatible sex drives and a mutually satisfying physical connection—your emotional connection might become too strained to survive.

It might seem ridiculous to be thinking about these fundamentals when you're meeting someone for a drink for the first time, but I think it's important to put the first date in context, and to see that these things apply just as much to a first date as to a great relationship.

Why?

On a first date, mutual respect is very important. Without it, your date might be late and not even apologize, they might be un-

derdressed or scantily dressed, or they might behave inappropriately or rudely to you or to others. Similarly, without respect in your
heart, you won't have the kindness to give your date the fair chance
they deserve and be more accepting of their flaws and imperfections.

A sense of humor on a first date is very important. Without it
you might not be able to overlook his bad shoes or her bad hair, the
slow service at a restaurant, his or her jerky behavior, or the disappointment you feel if you think the date has been a waste of time.
Because, let's face it: there's a lot of bad hair and bad shoes out
there, and there are a lot of jerks, and if you can't come home and
laugh about a lousy first date you're going to have a hard time staying out there looking for love.

And while you're not supposed to have sex on a first date (or on
a second or on a third!) you need to know that there's a potential for
chemistry, physical or emotional, and ideally both—even if it's not
obvious the minute you lay eyes on each other.

THE IMPORTANCE OF CHEMISTRY

Speaking of chemistry, the question of chemistry—what it is,
whether you have to have it in a successful relationship, how much
is enough, and what you're supposed to do if you don't feel any
with another person—is one of the most important dating issues for
my clients and probably for you as well.

Those of you who have felt chemistry with another person—and
most of us have—know that it's a combination of physical attraction, emotional attraction, and spiritual attraction that combines in
some mysterious way that you can't always articulate. Chemistry
isn't about looks. It's about energy, a feeling of electricity between
two people that makes them want to be together: to talk, to touch,
and to connect on a deep level.

When I'm matching clients, it's impossible for me to know for
certain if two people are going to click that way—if they're going to
have that kind of natural attraction and instant chemistry that
makes a first date exciting. But instant chemistry isn't my intention
anyway, because I'm trying to make a real match, a long-term
match, not just setting two people up for a booty call.

SIX IS THE MAGIC NUMBER

When it comes to dating and finding love, I believe the average couple should have six or seven dates before they know whether it's going to work or not. Sitting down with someone for the first time makes people nervous, and that nervousness can overshadow and camouflage the true chemistry and compatibility underneath. Which is why I really encourage people to keep going and have those six dates before they give up and say *no way.*

Chemistry doesn't always happen on the first date, and while my clients always have the right to say that they didn't feel an attraction on a date and that the chemistry wasn't there, I always remind them that they need to be patient: sometimes chemistry takes time to develop.

Whether on the first date or after six, however, chemistry sometimes just isn't reciprocal. Just because you feel chemistry doesn't mean the other person feels it, too.

Sometimes in my role as a matchmaker, I'll talk to a man after he's gone on a date (or several) with the woman I've matched him with and he'll say, "Oh, I really liked her, Patti, she's a doll and I'd really like to see her again." And then I'll talk to the woman and she'll say, "No way, he's just not my type, Patti. Nice guy and all, but no chemistry." It's my job to call him back and say, "I'm sorry that you really liked her, but she just didn't feel the chemistry."

Many people confuse chemistry with physical attractiveness. They come in, sit down, and if they're not instantly impressed by the person I've set them up with they quickly decide it isn't a good match. She wanted someone with hair, and I set her up with a guy who's balding, or he wanted a Vegas showgirl and I set him up with someone who's cute and curvy. When they call me the morning after the date and tell me their complaints, I don't even bother trying to hide my annoyance.

Get over yourself! I'll tell them. *And stop being such a Shallow Dater!* Love isn't a beauty contest. Chemistry isn't just about looks or lack of looks or whether you're a size 5 or a size 14. Remember: sexy comes from the inside out.

Chemistry is about how you feel when you're with that person. It's about energy.

And that energy is what we often think of as chemistry.

But as I mentioned above, there's another kind of chemistry besides red-hot fire-engine instant attraction chemistry.

There's emotional chemistry, too.

Emotional chemistry is the connection you feel and the attraction you feel when, after you've spent the first ten seconds of the date gauging your level of physical attraction, or seeming lack thereof, you feel something click.

You walk in, you sit down, and maybe the guy you're meeting is average looking. But then you start to talk to him, and he turns out to be an 8 or a 9 because he's fabulous. He's kind. He's wonderful. And before you know it you're finishing each other's sentences.

We live in a physical world which means that visual impressions, especially in dating—and especially for men—are extremely important. A good visual impression might not get you the relationship of your dreams after the first date, but it almost certainly will get you past the first to a second or third date. Likewise, a bad visual impression will almost certainly disqualify you on the first date and blow your chances for a second date.

On that first date, you don't have much time to make a first impression: you've got maybe ten seconds to pass a physical inspection and ten seconds for your date to pass your physical inspection of them.

After that initial instant impression, you have about thirty minutes to pass the test for emotional chemistry with that other person when you decide whether all the factors that go into connecting with someone romantically—physical attraction (or at least the lack of repulsion), intellectual and spiritual and lifestyle commonalities—are combining in a positive way.

This half hour that comes after the shock of the initial impression is very important, which is why I always advise clients to take those thirty minutes to give someone a chance.

Because if you take that time, which really isn't very long, with every person you meet (except for the Internet liars) you will, eventually, find true love.

CRITERIA FOR SELECTING DATES

One very important but often overlooked aspect of dating is how you choose your dates.

Assuming, that is, that you do indeed choose your dates, instead of always waiting for them to choose you.

Clay, a recent client, was a great guy—terrific-looking and sensitive and well on his way to a financially stable future at thirty-one—but he came to me because he had yet to find "the one" and was frustrated by his lack of dating success. Some of the women he'd gone out with were younger, sometimes as much as ten years younger. Most of them had complicated situations—two women he'd gone out with were very recently divorced and had young children, and another was unemployed and having big money problems. I gave Clay credit for being game enough to date women with all kinds of interests and backgrounds—he certainly was living by my rule to be openminded and flexible about dating types—but it occurred to me to ask him about his selection process. I needed to know what he considered when saying yes or no to a potential date.

He hesitated for a few seconds and then said, "Well, I don't really pick them. They pick me."

I can't tell you how many clients—men and women—have said exactly the same thing and have made this mistake, and I can't emphasize enough how much this will affect your chances for success in dating. Selecting who you're going to go out with, get to know, and possibly become emotionally and physically involved with is the first and foremost aspect of dating, and being passive about it leaves you vulnerable to becoming a pawn in someone else's game. That's not a position you want to put yourself in.

While you want to be open to as many different types of people as possible when you're out there dating, it's crucial that you have a clear sense of the most basic and nonnegotiable requirements for who you will date and who you won't date.

Before I even sit down with a client—before I even bother to bring them in to my office and interview them—I prescreen them over the phone to make sure they fulfill all of my basic requirements. Each requirement might seem completely obvious to you as a dater, but you'd be surprised how many people decide to get involved with someone who has commitment issues or who is otherwise unavailable.

Make a note of these requirements and make sure that every person you consider dating at least meets these minimum standards, and preferably exceeds them.

The Four Seemingly Obvious Nonnegotiable Absolute Minimum Basic Requirements for Accepting Clients and Dates:

- Person must be single
- Person must be employed
- Person must be looking for an exclusive relationship, though not necessarily for marriage
- Person must be ready for a relationship, which means they must be emotionally, legally, and physically disconnected from their last serious relationship

DATING DON'TS

Let's get the don'ts out of the way first, because they're simple, basic, and obvious. At least you'd think they would be simple, basic, and obvious.

But the reason people come to me and the reason you bought this book is that they're not.

Acceptable behavior in life and in dating has, for some reason, become blurred to the point where people don't know and don't understand what's okay and what's not okay to do in social situations. We've become a culture of overthinkers and overanalyzers and, just as with common sense, our ability to conduct ourselves in public and with other people has diminished to the point where we need to be taught how to behave.

Which is why we're both here.

Understanding what not to do on a date is just as important as learning what you should do—because if you continue to do what you shouldn't be doing, you're going to undermine all your efforts to find love.

What follows is a very basic list of Dating Don'ts.

Study it.

Memorize it.

And follow it.

If you do, you'll increase your potential for succeeding at dating a hundredfold.

Dating Don'ts

- Don't do shots of tequila or down four martinis on the first date. Getting wasted on the first date usually doesn't lead to a second date.
- Don't bring in your territory. It's completely inappropriate to have your best friend or coworkers "accidentally" run into you at the bar or restaurant to check out your date and give you their stamp of approval.
- Don't interview your date. They're not on trial and you're not hiring them for a job. Instead of grilling your date, you need to make adult conversation.
- Don't compare your date to the checklist in your head or on a long piece of paper in your pocket.
- Don't forget your date's name. If you have trouble with names, say your date's name ten times before you leave your house so that you'll remember it when you get there.
- Don't get tongue-tied. If you have trouble with shyness, read the paper, watch the news, and come up with a list of five safe topics to talk about.
- Don't look for a compliment. Pay one instead.
- Don't interrupt your date or do all the talking. Remember that it takes two people to have a conversation, not just one self-absorbed blabbermouth.
- If you're trying to find Mr. Right, don't look for him in a bar.
- If you think you've found Mr. Right, don't go home with him (or bring him home) for six dates.

- If you are instantly disappointed in your date because you don't find them at all attractive, don't let your disappointment show. If you can't be kind and give them a chance anyway, then at least be nice. Treat your date as a business acquaintance and behave with tact and good manners.
- If you are instantly attracted to your date, don't suggest getting a hotel room and don't talk about how you want to have children with them.
- Don't get stuck. Prepare an exit strategy before the date: have a time you need to be home, or have a friend call you on your cell phone after half an hour to check in and give you an out if you need one.
- Don't chew with your mouth open, talk with your mouth full, or hold your fork like a toothbrush. Understand—or learn—basic table manners.
- Don't wipe your nose on your sleeve. Carry tissues and use them.
- Don't smoke on your way to the date. You don't want to show up smelling like an ashtray.
- Don't talk on your cell phone, return a page, or answer a text message on your BlackBerry.
- Don't brag about your house, second house, car, boat, motorcyle, snowmobile, all the money you have, all the people you've slept with, or how important you think you are.
- Don't flirt with anyone except your date. Men especially should be careful not to flirt with the bartenders and waitresses. Being nice can sometimes be mistaken for flirting, and women are very sensitive to this.
- Don't overdress or underdress—know the restaurant that you and your date are going to and dress accordingly.
- If you take medication, take it before the date instead of during the date. Your date shouldn't know your medical or psychological issues during the first hour of conversation.
- If you can't say anything nice, don't say anything at all.

DATING DO'S

Now that we've identified the don'ts, it's time to clarify the Dating Do's—the right things to do before and during a date to make sure you have the best chance of finding love. Committing this list to memory, too, will have a huge impact on improving your dating skills and improving your chances of finding true love.

Dating Do's

- When setting up the first date, spend no more than five minutes on the phone. You want there to be an air of mystery and you want to have a lot to talk about on the actual date. Don't risk running out of things to say because you've already said them during three hours on the phone and twenty text messages and e-mails.
- Guys should make the initial call and suggest where to have the date because it shows initiative. Guys should also pay for the first date. It might sound sexist and old-fashioned, but sometimes traditions become traditions for a reason. This is one of those times.
- Early evening is a great time for dates. Morning reminds us too much of work, and lunch is too informal and too rushed, since most of us have to get back to work. Early evening allows you the opportunity, if you do like each other, to have more time together.
- The best places to meet for a first date are public places. Restaurants are safe. Don't go to the movies or to secluded, quiet places where the pressure of forced intimacy or the creep factor can make you uncomfortable.
- Stay away from bars and clubs. There are too many people and too much activity; it's too loud and too distracting and it may cause you or your date to lose focus.
- Stay away from bookstores, too. Bookstores are where you meet, not where you date.
- A first date should never be a coffee date. It's the too-direct eye contact that makes women uncomfortable, and all that caffeine can make you jumpy. Try a nice restaurant or take a walk and talk.
- You have ten seconds to make a first impression, so look your best.

- Dress casual but nicely: don't wear sneakers or sweats. But don't wear a ball gown or a tux, either.
- Less is better when it comes to jewelry, which goes for both men and women.
- Less is better when it comes to makeup and fragrance, too. Which goes for both men and women.
- More is better when it comes to clothing: belly buttons, extreme cleavage, bra straps, thongs, butt cheeks, butt cracks, and tramp stamps should not be visible on a first date. But that doesn't mean you have to wear a business suit and keep your shirt buttoned up to your neck. A little cleavage is fine. Just remember that a little sexy goes a long way.
- Make sure to carry—and use—breath mints.
- Be yourself. Trying too hard to impress a date can be worse than underimpressing them.
- Show that you can be sexy, intelligent, and beautiful all at once. Don't be afraid to show all your strengths and assets. Show your sense of humor, smile, and make great eye contact.
- And, most important, be on time! Nothing makes you look worse than being late to a first date.

HOW TO END THE DATE

Getting closure at the end of a first date is always one of the hardest parts of dating. How you end your first date with someone (and later on, your second and third dates) depends, of course, on whether you want to see the person again and whether they want to see you again.

Like most things in life, learning how to end a date—with the hopes of seeing the person again or of never seeing the person again—takes practice. In order to do it successfully you're going to have to combine honesty, tact, and kindness.

Asserting yourself—being direct without being rude—is the best thing you can do; keeping people hanging is the worst thing you can do. If you say you'll call or e-mail the person the next day, do so. Otherwise, don't say it. If you don't want to see the person again, shut the door completely so that you don't lead them on and give them false hope. Saying something like this at the end of the date or in an e-mail or voice mail the next day will make things clear and allow both of you to move forward on your journey to find love:

"It was really great meeting you, and you seem terrific, but to be honest I just didn't feel the chemistry. Good luck in your search."

12

Getting Past the First Date

Let's Talk About What You're Not Going to Talk About

Everyone has a story.

What happened to them last week.

What happened to them last year.

What happened to them on the way to their date.

People love to tell their stories and most of the time their stories accomplish exactly what they're supposed to: they can make people laugh, they help people understand who you are and where you're coming from, and they can break the ice. And let's face it, when you're sitting across the table from a complete stranger for the first time on a date, it can feel like you're in Antarctica.

But basic everyday slice-of-your-life stories aren't the kinds of stories I'm worried about you telling someone on a date—someone you barely know who you're hoping will like you enough to want to see you again on a second date.

Or at least not be completely freaked out by you.

The kind of stories I'm worried about are the ones people tell about their pasts.

Depressing stories about their depressing childhoods and breakups.

Unflattering stories about how much of a disaster they are when it comes to dating.

Stories about the ailments they have and what they like to do in the bedroom.

For some reason, all too often, people feel compelled to tell their life story—to blurt it out piece by unflattering, unappealing piece—the minute they sit down with someone they don't know. It's as if a green light goes on in their head and all the normal conversational boundaries they follow in their regular life suddenly disappear.

But those boundaries shouldn't disappear.

If anything, at this early make-or-break stage of things, those boundaries should be reinforced.

Sitting down across from someone for the first time—whether you're at a business lunch or on a first date—is not the time to spill your guts.

Or the time to confess all your strange habits or hobbies or past experiences. Or to blurt out all the least appealing aspects of your personality.

Newsflash: a date is not a therapy session.

And a date is not the place to talk about your therapy sessions, either.

Dating is about getting to know another person, and about someone getting to know you. But that getting-to-know-you isn't supposed to happen all at once, in the first five minutes of meeting each other. It's supposed to happen slowly, over time, so that your personality and your core get a chance to unfold at a more gradual pace.

Sharing way too much information, way too soon, is a turnoff. Why? Because the person you're talking to doesn't know you yet. And because they don't know you yet they're not going to be able to process all the weird unflattering details that you're telling them, and they're not going to be able to see past it and like you in spite of it.

Nor should they be expected to.

BASIC OBJECTIVES FOR A FIRST DATE

Just so we're clear before we go any further, let's recap what you're trying to accomplish on a first date:

FIRST DATE 101: MAKING CONVERSATION

- When you are on a date, you only have about thirty minutes to build some sort of emotional chemistry. Do not waste time having long conversations about your children, pets, crazy hobbies and interests, or past relationships—a definite *do not*.
- Make sure the conversation is not all about you. Ask questions. Make sure you are listening when they are answering. Make sure you ask questions as much as you answer them. Remember, the art of communication comes in two forms: talking and listening.
- Stay away from politics and religion. These subjects are too intense for a first date. If one comes up during the date, change the subject. Try to keep conversation light and fun.
- Men need to know that women are turned off if you brag about your career, possessions, and especially other women. A woman also likes a man who can be sensitive. Show a bit of your softer side.
- Do not talk about your sex life . . . past, present, or what you would like in the future. Leave it in the bedroom where it belongs.
- Do not use an excessive amount of foul language on a first date. It's a huge turnoff.
- Do not talk about tough family wounds, history, or sadness.
- Do not talk about your physical or emotional health. That is your private business.

- To learn something about the other person
- To assess whether you feel physical chemistry, or emotional chemistry, or both—or neither
- To share enough about yourself with the other person so that they can learn something about you
- To have fun
- To make a new friend
- To not blow your chances for a second date if you feel physical or emotional chemistry with the person or think there's a chance you could in the future

DON'T BLURT!

Take Tammy, a cute, thirty-four-year-old web designer who had three dogs, four birds, and more cats than I care to remember. She was so into animals that sometimes over the weekend her pets were the only "people" she talked to.

It was clear that there was a story behind the Noah's Ark that Tammy had created in her home—and the short version is that she felt safe with animals in a way she didn't feel safe with people. She'd created a surrogate family of animals who she could love and who would love her back, and it didn't take Jane Goodall to know that it was interfering with her dating life.

Her menagerie was a red flag the size of Texas.

Which is why I told her that when I sent her out on dates she was going to have to follow my rule and keep the animal talk to a minimum.

Don't go there, I said.

And for the first part of the first date she didn't.

Even when her date mentioned that he liked horseback riding, she resisted the urge to bring up her animals.

But just when it looked as if they'd made it past the subject, her date asked her if she had any pets. It was the moment of truth, and instead of following my advice and keeping her Animal Planet out of the date, she broke my rule and sang like a canary.

Tammy's dogs and cats and birds were out of the bag.

But it got even worse later, when her date took her home. Walking into her house, he not only saw all her animals, he even saw Tammy talking to them, calling them by their names, and telling each of them that she loved them.

It didn't take long for him to cut the drop-off short and run away from the wild kingdom inside her house because he was completely freaked out.

Then there's Patrick—a tall, blond, handsome, and hardworking forty-four-year-old nice guy who'd been single for ten years by the time he came to me for help.

He also happened to still be a virgin.

Patrick had a story, too, and the short version had to do with the fact that he'd come from a tight but troubled Irish Catholic family. His parents fought a lot when he was a kid, and when they split up, he felt depressed and responsible for keeping his mother's mood up. In high school, despite being a good athlete who played baseball and football, he was a shy misfit with a nonexistent social life, and his lonely teenage years left him with a case of cripplingly low self-esteem. Even when he got his first girlfriend—when he was in his late twenties—things didn't go well in the sex department. He dated his next girlfriend in his thirties, but that didn't go much better: kissing was barely on the agenda, let alone actual sex. Patrick's big issue was his lack of self-confidence and to say it had gotten in the way of his dating life was an understatement.

I knew I wouldn't have any trouble matching Patrick—he had a great bod and was a good guy to boot—but I also knew one thing would get him into trouble: opening his mouth about his sex life. So just as I did with Tammy, I went over the ground rules:

I told him to pay attention to how much he talked and to what he talked about. I didn't want him talking about his virginity. Or the fact that the last time he'd french-kissed someone was ten years ago.

Only I said it a little more forcefully. I told him to *shut the fuck up!*

Because the fact that he was a virgin at forty-four wasn't cute; it was another red flag the size of Texas. And if he took it out and waved it around during a first date, the date would be over before it even had a chance to begin.

But just like Tammy, Patrick broke the rules, too.

Halfway into the first date I sent him on he brought up every detail of his past, including the fact that his first girlfriend had gone out with his roommate after they'd broken up, and that his relationship with his second girlfriend—who he was allegedly going to marry even though he'd never gotten past third base (who even says that anymore?)—didn't work out, either.

Not to mention the fact that he'd only had three other dates in his whole life and that he didn't go to his junior or his senior prom.

The excuses why his love life was pathetic were flying, and so was that giant red flag I'd warned him about. Before he had a chance to show his date some of the sweetness and true charm I'd seen in my office, she'd seen and heard enough. Even though he hadn't come out and actually said that he was a virgin, it was clear from everything he did say that there was something not right with his picture.

UNDERSTANDING WHY YOU BLURT

Most of the things people blurt out on first dates are inappropriate, ill-timed, and ill-advised. They are details that are much too personal—and usually also much too unflattering—to share with someone you don't know and who you're trying to impress.

Or at least, trying not to repel.

And even though most people who blurt aren't doing it on purpose and usually don't even know they're doing it, it doesn't matter. Blurt out the fact that you're a closet eater or you've been fired from every job you've ever had or you're estranged from your kids before the waitress has even taken your drink order, and chances are you're well on your way to blowing the first date, not to mention blowing your chances for a second date.

People talk too much for lots of reasons—because they're nervous, because they're out of practice socially, because they haven't been on a date in twenty years and they have no idea what to talk about and how to behave. Sometimes it's ego that makes them talk too much; other times it's just that they like the sound of their own voice. But whatever the reason, it has to be fixed.

Part of what I work on with my clients one on one and what we've been working on here in this book focuses on how to be more comfortable—or less uncomfortable—on dates, so that you become better and better at dating. The less nervous you are, the less likely you are to blurt out every last detail of your romantic résumé or the long list of things your kids won't eat.

But nervousness and social awkwardness aren't the only reasons people become blurters on dates.

What makes a lot of people tell too much about themselves too soon is that they feel the need to be honest. To be completely up-front about anything and everything they think their date has a right to know about them. Anything less than 100 percent full disclosure about their past and present and they feel they're being dishonest and deceptive.

Wrong.

And while lying about yourself—in person or online—is wrong, selling yourself isn't like selling a used car.

And dating isn't a legal transaction.

I tell clients to be vague. Being vague doesn't mean you're lying. It's a perfect way to practice the "Less Is More" Rule of limiting what you say and when you say it.

No one has a right to know everything about you—especially so early in the game—and you don't have a right to know everything about them. In fact, the fewer intimate details you know about someone and the less they know about you the better, because it will give you both a chance to relax and see if there's any chemistry—physical or emotional—between you.

It will also give the person a chance to like you. And once someone likes you they're more able to process and accept the more complicated parts of you and your story.

Another thing that makes people blurt out their entire life story before the beer and wings hit the table is that they believe when someone asks them a question, they have to answer it.

Wrong again.

Unless your first date is with a cop—who's on duty—you don't have to answer anything.

Now, don't get me wrong: just because I'm telling you to be careful about how much you tell someone about yourself on a first or second date doesn't mean I'm telling you to misrepresent yourself, or to trick someone into liking you, or to lie.

All I'm saying is that getting to know each other doesn't mean getting to know every single detail about each other in the first five minutes of meeting. If you go slowly, there will be more dates and more time to reveal more parts of yourself.

I believe in the honesty-is-the-best-policy philosophy—that hiding your true self or pretending to be someone you're not is no way to go through dating, much less to go through life.

I believe that being true to who you are and getting to your core are absolute necessities in the quest for finding—and keeping—love.

So believe me when I say that talking too much early on in the dating process about the issues I outlined above is a sure way to fail at dating. And if you fail at dating, you're never going to find love.

The consequences of blurting early in dating can be irreparable. Blurting makes your date nervous and uncomfortable. It makes them want to get away from you as soon as possible. For example, why would someone admit to a stranger on a first or second date that their husband cheated on them or didn't want to have sex with them for the last three years—or both? Telling that to someone you've just met would instantly kill whatever chemistry there might have been.

The more overly personal and confessional you get, the more they're going to want the date to end, and if that's what they're thinking then the date is already over. Because across the table they'll no longer see you—an attractive, interesting, sensitive potentially dateable woman. Instead, what he's seeing across the table is a big red flag.

You are now *someone with issues* and *someone with issues* is a red flag the size of Texas.

Red flags are not good things to see during a date, no matter which side of the table you're on. Red flags scare people off, freak them out, and generally shut down the possibility of there ever being a second date.

Causing a red flag to appear is the ultimate disqualifier and one of the most common obstacles to successful dating. A red flag screams *issues,* and one of the least attractive things in a person is having a lot of issues.

Red flags lead to more red flags, and often it's the secondary red flag that's worse than the first. For example, one of the most common mistakes people make in dating is bad-mouthing an ex: an ex-boyfriend or ex-girlfriend, an ex-husband or ex-wife. Not only is the primary red flag—the too-much-information-on-a-first-date flag—a turnoff, but the secondary red flag is an even bigger turnoff. Bad-mouthing an ex is not only self-serving and unattractive, it can signal even more problems: that you're overly critical, that you're unable to take responsibility for your role in why the relationship failed, that you're unkind and nasty and unforgiving.

PATTI'S RED FLAGS THE SIZE OF TEXAS

Here are a few red flags to watch out for:

- Your date still lives at home with his family after the age of thirty.

- Your date is still a virgin after the age of thirty-five.

- Your date tells you they haven't had a date since high school.

- Your date is rude to the waitress.

- Your date flirts with the waitress.

- Your date suggests you split the check the first time you go out.

- Your date holds a fork like a toothbrush.

- Your date looks like they need a toothbrush.

GETTING OVER THE URGE TO BLURT

Obviously the point of dating is to get to know someone and to let them get to know you—but it doesn't all have to happen all at once, all on the first date, all before you've finished the first drink.

Casual conversation is the best way to get to know someone early on, and the best way to get a true sense of who they are and what they're like. The stories they tell you about their day, the stories they tell you about where they grew up, about what they love to cook and what their favorite movies are—these are what you should be talking about and asking them about, not why they think their marriage broke up or why they haven't dated since.

So how do you fight the urge to blurt?

How do you remind yourself not to go there and to keep away from certain topics and subjects that are better saved for later?

Here are a few basic tips to help you avoid the pitfalls of saying certain things that should be left unsaid—at least, for now.

1. *The "Less Is More" Rule.* One of the easiest ways to avoid one of the biggest dating mistakes is to follow the "Less Is More" Rule. The less you tell someone—the fewer ultrapersonal details you share about yourself with someone you barely know—the less turned off and more intrigued they'll be. When in doubt, be vague. Tell your date too much and they'll have had enough by the time the evening is over. Follow the "Less Is More" Rule and you'll leave them wanting to know more about you, not wishing they knew less.

2. *The Onion Rule.* In order to stick to the "Less Is More" Rule, think of yourself and your story like an onion—something that is made up of many layers. Before you go on your date, think of pulling back only a few of those outer layers of your personality—the most basic layers—on this first date. See all those other layers? They shouldn't be pulled back until the second date. Or the third date. Or the tenth date. Which, if you follow the Onion Rule, you'll have a good chance of getting to.

3. *The Turtleneck Trick.* My father used to say that there was "nothing like a woman in a turtleneck." It was his version of the "Less Is More" Rule, and it's the ultimate metaphor for maintaining an air of mystery. Now, of course, my father was talking about women—*me*—literally wearing turtlenecks as opposed to other more revealing kinds of clothing, but I couldn't agree more with his point as it extends to what you talk about. Wearing a turtleneck obviously means that you're not showing off everything right away—that there are some things (like your cleavage, for instance) that are going to be left to the other person's imagination. Figuratively, it means—or should come to mean—that you don't have to tell a person you've just met every single thing about yourself. Some things can be left to the imagination and be private for the time being.

4. *Limit the Alcohol.* One of the reasons people talk too much on dates is because they drink too much. Limit the drinking on your first date and you'll find that it's a lot easier to keep away from off-limits topics.

5. *Limit the Time.* Another enemy in the war against blurting is having too much airtime to fill up. That's why I tell people to talk on the phone for no longer than five minutes prior to a date and then to keep the first date itself short—an hour.

6. *Don't-Tell-Even-If-You're-Asked Policy.* The military has the ultimate don't-ask-don't-tell policy. And that's definitely a policy to follow on early dates. But a variation on that theme is equally important. Often times, when I debrief a client to find out why they blurted during a date when I'd told them not to—and when they themselves were prepared to follow my advice—they'll say it's because their date asked them. My rule for dealing with a too-direct question on a date is this:

Even if someone asks you, don't tell. *Yet.*

Again, when in doubt, leave things vague.

Some people find this very hard to do. They either have a hard time coming up with a comeback, or they can't think of a way to change the subject, or they don't want to be rude. Part of being a good date, they think, is being polite and answering anything and everything they're asked.

Let's go back to Tammy with all the pets.

Instead of saying she had three dogs, four birds, and a bunch of cats when her date asked her if she had any pets, she could have been vague and just said this:

"Yes, I love animals."

If he asked her what kind of pets she had, she could have said:

"I have dogs."

If he persisted and said, "Like, two?" she could have been vague again and said:

"I have a few dogs. I love animals."

End of conversation. And time for a new topic.

Here's another example:

Let's say Patrick the Virgin's date had started grilling him about his relationship history, trying to get to the bottom of why a nice guy like him was still single at forty-four. All he had to do was say:

"I've just never found the right girl."

If pressed by a follow-up question, he could have offered: "Things just haven't worked out yet."

Again, end of conversation. And time for a new topic.

7. *Just Say No.* One of the easiest rules to remember when someone asks you a question you don't want to answer is that you have the option of not answering it. It seems simple, but if it were, I wouldn't have had to make up the Don't-Tell-Even-If-You're-Asked Policy we just went over. But you have the right to just say no to answering overly invasive questions and to put a stop to any conversation topic that makes you uncomfortable. If subtle evasion or changing the subject or making your answers vague doesn't shut your date down, it's time to be direct and to stop mincing words. If your date asks you point-blank why you got divorced and you don't feel like answering, a firm "It's none of your business" or "Why do you want to know?" or even "It's complicated—as these things always are—and I'd really rather not talk about it now" will usually get your message across.

8. *Don't Ask Anyone Anything You Wouldn't Want to Answer Yourself.* This is one of those rules that seem completely obvious because it should be common sense—but you'd be amazed how many people are clueless when it comes to cross examining their dates. If there are things you don't want to talk about or questions you don't want to answer, don't bring them up or ask your date about them. Women: stop asking your dates how many girlfriends they've had. Men: stop grilling your dates about what they like to do in the bedroom. Chances are, even if they submit to your questions, you're not going to want to hear their answers.

TRY-THIS-AT-HOME EXERCISE

Just to make sure you understand all the concepts we've covered in this chapter—and in the rest of the book—here's one last exercise: a true or false quiz. If you've been paying close attention all along and have completed the previous worksheets and exercises, this should be easy.

If it isn't, you might want to go back and reread and review things.

WAYS TO PRACTICE SAFE CONVERSATION

Go into your first date with a few topics in mind to talk about and a few light interesting questions to ask your date. Topics like music, hobbies, and work usually are good places to start. When it's time for a little more background, steer the conversation to funny stories about your siblings or growing up in your family and ask your date to do the same.

Because getting over yourself, like finding true love, is a process that takes some people more time than others.

Part of getting over yourself is becoming more aware of your behavior so that you can begin to change it. In this exercise, think about a date you went on where you think you may have turned your date off by revealing too much about yourself and causing some red flags to go up.

Note: If you're not sure whether or not you put your date off, if you answer yes to any of these questions, you did.

- Your date got that distant, glazed, zoned-out look on their face while you were talking.
- Your date looked uncomfortable during certain parts of your story. He may have even actually cringed at points or said, in a seemingly joking fashion that wasn't actually joking, that you were giving him "too much information."
- That date did not lead to a second date.

PATTI'S "HAVE YOU GOTTEN OVER YOURSELF BY UNDERSTANDING THAT LESS IS MORE WHEN IT COMES TO TELLING YOUR LIFE STORY ON THE FIRST DATE?" SELF-TEST

1. The more I reveal about myself to a date early on, the better, since it shows I'm an honest and forthcoming person and that I have nothing to hide.

       TRUE   FALSE

2. The purpose of casual dating is to find out as much about the other person as possible—better to weed out the bad apples sooner rather than later.

TRUE   FALSE

3. Patti says I should think of the layers of my personality as being like the layers of an onion and that I should keep a picture of an onion in my head to remember her rule about peeling back these layers during dates. The picture I should have in my head of that onion should look like one of those deep-fried "bloomin'" onions, with all the layers pulled back all at the same time, right?

TRUE   FALSE

4. Patti's Turtleneck Trick says that the best way to create an air of mystery about yourself is to always wear a turtleneck on a first or second date.

TRUE   FALSE

5. Patrick the Virgin should have just come right out and told his date that he was a virgin. His date had a right to know that something was a little off about him.

TRUE   FALSE

6. Tammy's date should have tried to get to the bottom of why she was so obsessed with animals and why she felt safer with her pets than with people.

TRUE   FALSE

7. While it's interesting to try to figure out why I blurt, the more important thing is to stop blurting.

TRUE   FALSE

8. Telling self-deprecating stories about myself makes people laugh, makes me more likable, and is a good way for me to break the ice.

TRUE   FALSE

9. Drinking on a first date is good because it helps me loosen up and be less uptight.

TRUE   FALSE

10. The less I reveal about myself on a first date, the more likely I am to have a second date.

TRUE   FALSE

Answers:

1. *False.* The more you reveal about yourself to a date early on, the worse you look, since it shows that you don't have a clear sense of social boundaries and what constitutes appropriate conversation. People who do have a clear sense of boundaries and appropriate conversation are people who are more emotionally healthy. And people who are more emotionally healthy make better dates and better mates.

2. *False.* The purpose of casual dating is not to treat your date like they're on trial. It's to have fun and to make a new friend. Cross-examine your date like they're a criminal with something to hide and you probably won't ever see them again.

3. *False.* Think of yourself as a regular onion—the kind that hasn't "bloomed" yet and where all the layers are still intact until you start pulling them back slowly, one at a time, date by date by date.

4. *False.* Don't get all smart-alecky. Just remember the point of the turtleneck: Less is more.

5. *False.* First of all, Patrick's date doesn't have a "right" to know anything about him. And second of all, *newsflash:* Patrick the Virgin's date knew there was something "a little off" about him even without him going all the way and blurting out the fact that he was a virgin.

6. *False.* Asking general questions about Tammy's pets was one thing, but if Tammy's date had started probing and asking sensitive questions about why she had so many, she certainly would have gotten uncomfortable. And if she'd actually answered those questions—and gotten into ultrasensitive personal territory that quickly—her date would have been uncomfortable, too.

7. *True.* While it's interesting and helpful to understand the root of self-defeating behaviors like blurting, it's more important to learn how to stop behaving in self-defeating ways. Because until you stop doing those things, you're not going to be able to find love.

8. *False.* I don't care how big that ice floe you're on feels: do not put yourself down on a first date (or a second or a third). Talking unflatteringly about yourself shows that you don't like yourself and that you have low self-esteem, and low self-esteem is a red flag for lots of even bigger issues and problems. And red flags, issues, and problems are a big turnoff in the early stages of dating.

9. Having one drink—a glass of wine, a glass of beer—on a date is fine. Having ten drinks or doing shots of tequila is not.

10. *True.* End of answer.

THE SECOND DATE: WHY IT'S HARDER THAN THE FIRST DATE

So much of the work we've done throughout the book has been to prepare you for your big goal: getting ready to date and to find love. And so much of what I hope you've learned in the book is what will help you get through that first date successfully—successfully enough to make it to the second date.

So often people don't make it past the second date. Which is why you have to pay attention to the second date, because it could be the last.

As a rule, the second date is much harder than the first date because it's longer, which usually means dinner and more conversation. Navigating those decisions (where to go, where to meet, who pays) is a little trickier than the first date because you know each other a little bit better than you did on the first date and presumably like each other a little bit since you both agreed to see each other again.

There's also a greater opportunity for rejection because, while you think you've passed the inspection of the first date, you haven't necessarily. You have more invested by the second date and thus more to lose if it doesn't lead to a third date.

The second date is longer so it potentially involves more alcohol than the first. Which means you have to be especially careful not to drink too much and then talk too much (remember your common sense). The temptation is to really let your hair down—and your guard down—which gets a lot of people into trouble because they overshare and often come on too strong too soon. Keep the "Less Is More" Rule in effect throughout the second date. Sharing the good, the bad, and the ugly parts of the life you've led up until meeting your "new best friend"—your date—could ruin your chances.

Also, since the second date usually involves dinner, this is the time when you could find out your date has terrible table manners or is rude to the waitress (or flirts with the waitress). Behavior that didn't show itself on the first date, when both of you are showing your best side, often surfaces on the second date.

Trying to figure out whether you feel chemistry with your date yet—and whether you think you could feel it on a third or fourth or fifth date—can be distracting and can take your energy and attention away from the date itself. Try to stay focused and in the moment: relax, listen to what your date is saying, and keep the conversation positive and interesting. Save your complete assessment of the date for after the date.

HOW TO FIND A GOOD MATCHMAKER

If you've gotten to the end of this book and think that you want or need someone to help you find love, maybe it's time for you to get your own matchmaker!

There's been a surge of interest in matchmakers and matchmaking lately—and I'm not just saying that because I am one and because that's what I do. Matchmaking is a long-standing tradition in some cultures—Jewish and Chinese, to name only two—and that gives it a sense of legitimacy and validity other dating services don't have.

One reason so many people have turned to matchmakers recently to find love is because there are more singles today than ever before: 92 million unmarried Americans, according to 2006 U.S. Census Bureau figures. And the reason there are so many singles is because people are delaying marriage and staying single longer (the number of unmarried men and women in their thirties has tripled over the last thirty years), and the divorce rate is sky high at more than 50 percent.

Another reason for the interest in matchmakers is that all those single people feel frustrated by the lack of alternatives or the lousy alternatives they have when it comes to meeting other singles: they're tired of the bar scene and they're scared of Internet dating (and they should be). They're frustrated by not knowing where to look for quality potentials and how to make good dating choices.

Matchmaking is an alternative to no alternative. It gives you a professional to turn to who will help guide you to other high-quality single people who are also looking for love. If you're lucky, that matchmaker will also help you improve your dating skills so you stop repeating past mistakes and therefore increase your chances for success.

There's no magic or scientific formula for finding a good matchmaker, but if you're looking for one you need to be a careful consumer so that you find a person who is not only honest and reputable, but also has heart and good gut instincts about who to match you with. Keep these thoughts in mind when conducting your search for a matchmaker who's right for you.

- In order for a matchmaker to use those good instincts they have to know something about you, and that means the in-person interview you have with your prospective matchmaker is extremely important. The more they know about you, the better they'll be able to sort through their client base and find you matches that are at least in the ballpark of what you're looking for. Be honest and truthful with your answers. And if your prospective matchmaker asks you only the bare minimum of questions, you should probably continue your search for someone more curious about you and thorough in their approach.

- When you start your search, try a local matchmaker with a smaller company. That's not to say that bigger national matchmaking services can't be good, but an independent service will have a better understanding of the singles scene and more knowledge of people in your area.

- Just as it's important for the prospective matchmaker to do a thorough and in-depth interview with you to get to know you, it's important that you find out how the interviewer will actually be involved in helping you. If that person says that they will not personally be matchmaking for you, run the other way. Because it's likely that the clerical staff at the service will end up doing your matchmaking.

- It's crucial, too, to find out the size of the company's pool of prospects. If you're a thirty-eight-year-old woman, for instance, find out how many men the company has between twenty-seven and thirty-eight years old. Remember that a matchmaker is only as good as the quantity of quality clients they can match you with: whether or not they have been "certified" as a "professional matchmaker" is meaningless.

- Don't forget to honestly assess your dating and relationship skills. After reading this book, if you see yourself as someone who has trouble getting to a second or third date you should try to locate a lifestyle coach, too. They look at the whole being and will be able to help you with specific appearance issues (hair, clothing, makeup) and dating skills (making conversation, improving shyness, maintaining good eye contact). Sometimes you can find matchmakers who also provide coaching—the way I do—but often those two areas require separate specialists.

THE THIRD DATE AND BEYOND: FINAL THOUGHTS

One of the many things I've learned in all my years of being a matchmaker is this:

If you get to the third date, you'll likely get to ten dates. And that will put you in or close to a three-month relationship.

If this book has helped you see yourself more realistically and become more aware of what you need to work on in order to find love—the core issues you need to deal with or the communication skills and listening skills you need to develop, for instance—then you have a lot to be proud of. You've been brave enough to take a cold hard look at yourself and be honest and truthful with yourself about what you want—true love—and to start doing the hard work that it takes to find it.

And keep it.

Dating isn't a game. The way you behave with people you meet and how you interact with them—whether it's on the first date or the tenth date—isn't any different from how you should behave and interact with all the people in your life, which is what this book has really been about.

It's been about treating yourself and others with honesty and kindness and respect, and it's been about getting you to see yourself for who you really are: all the goodness inside of you, all the great parts of your personality and your character, while at the same time acknowledging some things you need to get over.

It's also been about making yourself vulnerable, no matter how much you've been hurt in your past and no matter how afraid you are of being hurt again in the future.

And the reason you need to get over your issues isn't because you're desperate and lonely and miserable—it's because when you're finally at peace with yourself you'll be ready, maybe for the first time in your life, to connect with someone in a healthy way. With that positive energy coming from your core—from your mind and your body and your soul—you will find the love and the happiness that you've always wanted and that you truly deserve.

So much about finding love is balance: understanding what we need to change and what we need to accept in ourselves and in others. And it's balance and a strong faith in yourself that will carry you through the last page of this book and into your new life.

Appendix 1

A Field Guide to Dating Tips

Figuring out what kind of dater you are and what type of dater you're most often attracted to is a key piece of getting over yourself. It's one of the most important parts of my in-depth interview with a new client, because before I can help them I need to know which category they fall into and which category most of the people they date fall into.

By watching a person's body language, looking at their clothes and how they groom themselves, and listening to what they say—or don't say—I can get a read on whether they are a narcissist or a wallflower, an optimist or a pessimist, a positive dater or a negative dater.

Does the client have an air of grandiosity and the attitude that I'm lucky to be talking to them?

Probably a Narcissistic Dater.

Does the client talk about all the pain and suffering they've endured throughout their life?

Probably a Sad-Victim Dater.

Or an Angry Dater.

Or a Blamer.

Am I falling asleep or flatlining listening to the client talk or getting exhausted trying to get the client to talk?

Definitely a Boring Dater.

Or an Awkward Dater.

Or a Shallow Dater.

Or a Social Misfit.

Some people might not like the idea of being labeled based on just a few behaviors or personality traits. People are individuals, after all, and shouldn't be reduced to stereotypes. And you know what I say to that?

Get over yourself!

It is what it is.

If you want to be successful in dating and if you want to find love, you have to have a clear and realistic picture of who you are.

Not who you *think* you are.

Or who you *hope* you are.

But who you *actually are.*

And if you're like most daters in the world, you probably fall into a category that is fairly common and identifiable.

Obviously, the categories I'm going to tell you about are not clinical definitions of personality types or behaviors. And obviously they're not 100 percent exact. Chances are that you or the people you know or the people you date will not fall into one discrete category. You'll probably fall into one or two or even three because many of these types overlap with other similar types.

The types I'm going to describe are the daters I've seen the most after years and years of matchmaking. They're probably types that you'll find easy to recognize, either because you see yourself in these descriptions or you see the people you've dated.

THE OFFICIAL UNOFFICIAL GUIDE TO DATING TYPES

The Angry Dater

Often a Blamer, sometimes a Classic Bitch, the Angry Dater is a veteran of bad relationships, bad divorces, bad jobs, bad childhoods. Angry Daters are overthinkers and overanalyzers who still have demons they have not faced and who have never gotten past the angry/blaming stages of their emotional development process. Women are more often Angry Daters than men because they generally have a harder time letting go of things like bad breakups or divorces, but there are plenty of men who are Angry Daters, too. Men are usually so good at burying the things that have hurt them deeply—like divorces or being cheated on—that they can almost forget about them, but all that repression takes energy and never quite eliminates the well of anger those painful experiences have created.

The Asshole

This category doesn't break down on gender lines, either: which is to say, an Asshole is an Asshole. Men are thicker, and women are bitchier, but at the end of the day they're still the most impossible and unpleasant and unsuccessful daters out there. Instead of wasting my time and yours with a description of such an obvious type, I have some advice for the Asshole: *Get over yourself!*

The Awkward Dater/The Social Misfit

Awkward Daters and Social Misfits are mostly men. They are painfully shy and have profound self-esteem issues. Unfortunately, most Awkward Daters and Social Misfits have never gotten counseling to help them be less anxious around women and, more important, to get to the heart of their deeply rooted insecurity.

If a very young man—twenty-one to twenty-five years old—is interested in my help, I know that he will most likely fall into this category. Either he's so mature from life experiences that he doesn't fit in with the people his age—he's twenty-two going on thirty-two, for instance—or his social awkwardness has stunted his emotional development and he is less mature than people his age. Either way, the Awkward Dater needs lots of help: probably a makeover for clothes and grooming and hairstyle, and dating lessons and continued coaching.

I've worked with quite a few clients who were Social Misfits, including Brian, who signed up with me twice. He was tall, dark, and handsome with a good job, but no matter who I matched him with he couldn't get past the first date. He was shy and awkward and made poor eye contact. He was argumentative, he talked too loudly, and he wouldn't listen. In the end, though he was (like most Social Misfits) a smart and tender guy, I couldn't help him, because his denial was stronger than his self-awareness.

Social Misfits are some of the most difficult people to help. They're incapable of communicating with the opposite sex in a healthy, direct fashion and instead mask it with an aggressive or twitchy or insecure manner, and are thus crippled when it comes to dating because their dates only see the mask of severe awkwardness, not the person behind it. The Social Misfit's problems run deeper than the Shy Dater's or the Nervous Talker's and are almost always attached to bigger emotional or psychological problems. Often they're suppressing dark issues in their life. The Social Misfit isn't beyond hope, but they should start with a good therapist and would do great with a female dating or life coach to help them get more comfortable with the opposite sex.

The Blamer

This type of person/dater blames everyone for everything—everyone except him- or herself, that is. The Blamer's problems are always someone else's fault: their ex-husband's, their ex-girlfriend's, their parents'. The real problem Blamers have is that they've never learned how to solve their own problems.

The therapy movement of the seventies and eighties encouraged people to figure out the source of their difficulties in life, but pinning the blame on others led to certain problems. Finding the root of your problems and identifying the culprits is fine and often useful, but some people were never given any tools for getting past that point of blaming: they were never instructed on how to get over themselves and their pasts in order to move on with their lives.

Blamers can't, don't, and won't take responsibility for themselves and their own actions and the outcomes of those actions, and they go through life with a sense of helplessness and immaturity. That helplessness in turn leaves them angry at the world because they feel like they have no control over their own destiny: they are simply victims of people who they blame for having all the control.

Blamers need to stop blaming other people for the fact that they haven't taken responsibility for their own lives, and they need to understand that until they do they won't be able to find love—and it won't be anyone's fault but their own.

The Boring Dater

How do you create energy around someone who has flatlined but is still alive? I don't know, so the Boring Dater is one of the hardest types to help through a first date. The good news is that if the Boring Dater can make it through a first date without boring their date to death, they can usually make it to a second date. The bad news is that if the Boring Dater is still really boring on the second date, it's unlikely that anyone will agree to sit through a third date with them.

The Childless Animal Lover

This type of dater is usually a woman, either never married or divorced, who has a passion for her pets. Not just dogs or cats. But dogs and cats she treats like children. Children she doesn't have. Whether she never wanted children, or wanted them but couldn't have them (not that there's anything wrong with not having children, mind you) she focuses all her maternal human love and attention on animals. Which can be just a little creepy if it goes too far—like, say, carrying photos of her "children" in her wallet and showing them to her date; or telling her ten birds, eight cats, and seventeen fish she loves them in front of her date; or never being able to make dinner plans or travel plans because she can't leave her "babies." The Childless Animal Lover finds it easier to connect with animals than with people, which can be a symptom of a much deeper and more serious problem with intimacy. At the very least, it can seem just odd enough to get in the way of finding love.

The Classic Bitch

This type of woman crosses several problematic categories—she's an Angry Dater wrapped up in a Narcissistic Dater's clothing. She's bossy, controlling, aggressive, and self-absorbed, not to mention rude, pushy, demanding, and ungracious. She's someone for whom happiness and contentment have always been elusive, or nonexistent. Often an overachiever, the Classic Bitch is never satisfied— with herself or anyone else. She desperately needs to get over herself if she's ever going to find love.

The Delusional Dater/The Overly Romanticizing Dreamer Dater

More women than men, this type reads too many love stories and goes to see too many foreign films. The result? A fantasized version of dating and relationships and a completely unrealistic sense of expectations when it comes to love and romance.

The Eccentric Dater

More often women than men, the Eccentric Dater is the woman with the wild hair, the giant earrings, and the pancake makeup. The woman who looks like she's either forty-two or sixty-two, and whose frumpy crazy look serves as the perfect protection from potential dates. The Eccentric Dater has low self-esteem and little self-confidence but can, with a few quick improvements, lose the weird look that kept her out of the dating scene for far too long.

The Exaggerator/The Embellisher

The Exaggerator always adds a little to the story they're telling—or takes something away from it—to make it more interesting and exciting. Like any liar—because that's essentially what the Exaggerator is—they always begin with a nugget of truth, but by the time they're done with their version of an event or an incident they've put themselves at the center of the story and done something epic and impressive that makes them sound like a superhero. Exaggeration and embellishing are symptoms of the Narcissistic Dater and all types of insecure daters who are beset by the feeling that whatever they say or do just isn't good enough, which is why they have to add to it and improve upon it.

Unfortunately, people almost always pick up on the fact that whatever the Exaggerator is saying isn't exactly the truth. Embellishing feels like lying because it *is* lying, and, while it comes from insecurity and a need to feel in control, it can be a complete deal breaker out in the dating world. If you didn't play for the Dallas Cowboys, don't say that you did, because whoever was the beneficiary of your embellishment will eventually find out that you're lying. Exaggerators need to get to the root of the demon that makes them feel less-than and understand that sticking to the truth—the whole truth and nothing but the truth—is the only chance they have of ever finding love, especially because Embellishers and Exaggerators really get into trouble on the third date and beyond.

The Extremely Picky Dater/The Forever Dater

Only about three out of ten people are open and flexible about who they're going to date. Most people have unrealistic expectations: they want things they can't have, or worse, they want things they themselves don't offer. Most picky daters have issues related to insecurity and fear. They have a long list of requirements of what they require in a date or a partner, which makes it almost impossible to match them, much less for them to ever settle on someone since no one could possibly make it through their ridiculous checklist. Not to mention the fact that the Extremely Picky Dater often has unrealistic expectations, like the clients who fill out one of my questionnaires and say they want a 10 when they're a 6 at best. Their pickiness is a defensive behavior, one they've acquired to avoid dating and intimacy, and it is almost always a sign of deep-rooted insecurity and fear. Inside most Extremely Picky Daters are Shy, Angry, Sad-Victim Daters, and sometimes even Social Misfits.

The main danger of being a picky dater is the risk of becoming a Forever Dater: someone who spends their life looking for something they can't find because they're not sure exactly what they're looking for or even why they're looking for it. While commitment issues are part of the Forever Dater's problem, at their core is a deep and fundamental confusion about who they are (and sometimes about their true sexual preference) and what, if anything—or anyone—will fill the emptiness inside them.

The Fifty-Three-Year-Old Virgin

Rare, but out there, the Fifty-Three-Year-Old Virgin is a second cousin to the "Is He Gay?" Dater, making us wonder if the reason this type is still a virgin has less to do with past breakups and insecurity and low self-esteem and more to do with confusion and unresolved issues surrounding sexual preference.

The Gold Digger

This type is as old as the hills, and despite the classic female version, these days the Gold Digger is just as often a man. Both sexes need to be on the lookout for this person who, obviously, is just looking for someone with money and means to support them and provide them with a very comfortable lifestyle, and not for true love.

The "Is He Gay?" Dater

We'd all be lying if we said we hadn't encountered this sexually ambiguous type at least once in our dating careers: the sort of man who is way more effeminate than we're comfortable with. He goes beyond the stereotypical traits and trappings of the new metrosexual (who's obsessed with fashion, style, fitness, and grooming) and isn't just someone who is in touch with his feminine side, which can be a great thing in a man. The "Is He Gay?" Dater gives off some sort of vibe that makes us think that even if the "Is He Gay?" Dater isn't gay, he might not be entirely straight.

The Lazy Dater

Sorry, guys, but most Lazy Daters are men. The Lazy Dater is known for his—you guessed it—laziness: the only women he meets are the ones he meets at work (and the women he dates must be Lazy Daters, too, not for nothing!) or in his apartment building. Sometimes the Lazy Dater is so lazy he dates his friends' old girl-friends and ex-wives.

I had one client who was such a lazy dater that he had to leave seven jobs—at seven different facilities where he was a physical therapist—because he kept dating his coworkers (and dating them unsuccessfully!).

The Lazy Dater doesn't put much more effort into the actual date than he puts into meeting the woman, so don't expect too much in terms of imagination or planning when it comes to getting together—much less staying together. After all, how can you expect that he'll be romantic and nurturing in a relationship when he's uninspired early on? Fear is one of the underlying issues with the Lazy Dater (as it is for most problematic daters), and so is self-centeredness. Lazy Daters are almost always underachievers, which really is no surprise since you have to be in it to win it and most Lazy Daters are too afraid to put themselves out there to look for love in a serious way.

The Mannequin

This is the woman with the too-dark fake-and-bake year-round tan and the inch-thick foundation and mascara and lip gloss. The Man-nequin's look does two things you don't want to do when looking for love: it makes her look like she's covering something up, and it makes her look like she's not real. The Mannequin has to stop gild-ing the lily and hiding behind her fake look if she wants to get over herself and find love.

The Martyr

This is the dater who is always talking about how much they want to date but can't because of how much they have to do for other peo-ple. Sometimes a Sad-Victim Dater or Blamer and almost always a

Procrastinator, there are a thousand reasons that the Martyr has been single for the past ten years and they all have nothing to do with them and everything to do with everyone else: if only the people in their lives weren't so needy, maybe they'd have time to focus on themselves and their search for love. You know what I say to Martyrs? I bet by now you can guess: *Get over yourself!* Stop blaming your lack of initiative or fear on everyone else and start taking responsibility for your own search for happiness and companionship!

The Mother Hen/The Girl Who Can't Flirt

The Mother Hen is the perpetual buddy—always the girl "friend" instead of the girlfriend. Mother Hens have low self-esteem, either because of a bad breakup or body issues, and they smother potential dates with their well-meaning but completely unsexy motherliness. They're classic enablers who find it easier to focus on others than think about their own need to take care of everyone else except themselves. Someone who always has to take care of and fix everyone else is often the oldest sibling in her family and probably was a caregiver to the younger children when they were growing up.

Mother Hens are sometimes sarcastic and aggressive, and almost always Shy or Angry or Sad-Victim Daters at their core, and very often they're attracted to gay men because it's a way to enjoy male companionship in a safe environment. Unfortunately, being a Mother Hen doesn't build a healthy core for a woman. Women are supposed to have sex, and the longer one goes as a Mother Hen, the more repressed she gets and the thicker her defensive exterior becomes. Which is why she has to take a chance on love or she'll never have it.

The Girl Who Can't Flirt is a cousin of the Mother Hen and the Shy Dater but with a crash course in hair flipping, conversation-making, and eye contact, she can quickly get the hang of things and get back in the dating game.

The Narcissistic Dater

Narcissists are charmers. They're also usually Blamers. And Embellishers. And they're almost always Shallow Daters. Not to mention Players and Party Boys and Classic Bitches. Narcissistic Daters are adults who never truly bonded with one or both parents; because of that they often grow up to be profoundly insecure. That insecurity is then masked by self-absorption and self-centeredness and turns into a real inability to connect with others on a deep level. You will almost certainly come into contact with this complicated and pervasive type of dater at some point in your dating experience, if you haven't already: one out of four women have dated malignant narcissists, the worst type of narcissist (women who are attracted to men with narcissistic traits have to learn to avoid them, which is a big part of their own journey, but that's another story).

It's very difficult to help narcissists date because they are so self-consumed and self-absorbed they have trouble seeing and relating to other people—a very important and very basic part of dating. Narcissists can often attract dates, but they have a lot of trouble getting to the second date or keeping a relationship going because of their shallowness, self-centeredness, and grandiosity. Narcissistic Daters have another big problem: they're often bad sexual partners because of their inability to care about and focus on the needs of others.

The Nervous Talker/The Interrupter

Nervous Talkers are socially insecure, poor listeners, and mask all their fear about being vulnerable by talking too much at the beginning of a date. But the true Nervous Talker/Interrupter doesn't stop talking when they start to feel comfortable on a date: they just keep talking.

There are few types that are more annoying than the Nervous Talker, who makes it almost impossible to have a conversation because they're always cutting in and talking over you. In my job, the most frustrating place to be is sitting across the desk from someone who won't stop talking when I'm trying to have a give-and-take conversation to get to know them. Imagine how frustrating it is to sit across from them on a date. If you're an Interrupter and you're reading this book, I have news for you: no one's going to love an excessive talker and an Interrupter because it's aggravating to not be listened to and it makes true connection impossible. When an Interrupter comes to see me as a potential client and interrupts me every time I try to ask a question, I'll say, "You don't shut up and half of what you say is unimportant." If they hear that and manage to not interrupt me afterward, I'll consider taking them on because it's likely that with a little coaching and hard work on their part to learn how to control their verbal impulses, I can help them improve their dating skills to the point where they can actually get through a date without completely pissing off the person they're sitting across from.

The Overachieving Woman

This type of woman is accomplished and successful in her career but is trying to please someone other than herself, usually her parents. That compulsion to please through achievement and success makes it impossible for her to have balance in her life, which is why this type of dater needs to get over her need to please others and focus on what she needs to do to find balance—and love—in her life.

The Oversexed Dater

This is the person who sleeps with dates way too often and way too soon. Players and Party Boys usually fall into this category, as do Party Girls and Party Moms. Almost always the Oversexed Dater has developed because of a broken heart. Second-time-arounders, who have just gone through divorces, will sometimes go a little crazy with one night stands and booty calls because there was either a lack of sex in the marriage or a lack of emotionally close sex in the marriage—they felt unwanted and unattractive and are now looking for some attention, excitement, and validation. Certain women who fit this type are promiscuous because they have always thought love was sex. Inside the Oversexed Dater is usually an Angry Dater or a Sad-Victim Dater—someone who hasn't yet gotten over psychic and emotional wounds, like a client who, on the second date, slept with each of the eighteen men I'd set her up with because she still had unresolved issues with her ex-husband.

The Party Girl/Party Mom

I've had a lot of clients who fit this description. Sometimes the Party Girl/Party Mom is a middle aged woman—almost always a second-time-arounder—who does shots to get drunk, picks up guys half her age, and doesn't understand why she looks ridiculous and sometimes even sad and pathetic. Other times it's women in their thirties who still cruise college bars looking to have fun with guys in their late teens. Dressing in an age-inappropriate way is usually a problem with these women, whether they have always been single or are divorced now with kids, and too much drinking is almost always a factor, too.

The Party Girl/Party Mom has to learn to act her age, and in order to do that she has to learn to feel good about her age. She also has to see that too much partying and too many booty calls will lower her self-esteem even more than it already is and will make finding love almost impossible.

The Plain Jane

The Plain Jane stands out in a fading-into-the-woodwork kind of way: she's the one with the drab hairstyle, the drab clothes, and no makeup. The one that makes people cock their heads and say, *Gee, with a less drab hairstyle and some less drab clothes and a little makeup, she'd look pretty good.* Most Plain Janes have issues with self-esteem, self-confidence, and self-worth—all in the low-to-zero range—and because of that most have very little experience with dating.

When a Plain Jane comes into my office and I ask her why she doesn't wear makeup, she'll often say she wants to be loved for who she is. It makes me wonder if it's arrogance or fear that makes her take so little care with her appearance, and I usually end up thinking that the Plain Jane simply doesn't want to call attention to herself because she's scared to be noticed.

The good thing about Plain Janes is that often when they get some guidance with their hair, makeup, clothing and some basic coaching they can make great strides and become very successful daters, because those small changes can make a big difference in their self-perception and self-esteem.

The Player

Sometimes called the Party Boy Dater, the Player is the guy who thinks he's all that and a bag of chips. He travels with a posse, loves the bar scene, and prides himself on how many bartenders know him by his first name and will get his favorite drink before he asks for it. Frequently narcissists, Players are also almost always Late Bloomers, overcompensating in their adulthood for being unpopular and awkward in their adolescence. It takes a lot of work to turn this type around and transform him into a serious dater. The Player has to be ready to change and has to *want* to change in order to be able to connect with women on more than just a superficial and obnoxious level.

The Procrastinator

Also known as Mr. Busy (or Ms. Busy), this is the dater who's always too overscheduled to date, to focus on love, to buckle down and do the things that need to be done in order to find love. Maybe it's her job ("After this project I'll join that dating service"). Maybe it's his kids ("As soon as softball season is over I'll get serious"). Maybe it's the thousand other things the Procrastinator fills their life with that make it "impossible" to focus on finding love.

Well, *newsflash:* the Procrastinator has to learn how to be proactive.

And in order to become proactive they have to decide to make dating a priority and stop hiding behind their busy schedules as an excuse for avoiding their personal lives.

The other thing Mr. or Ms. Busy needs to learn is how to stop talking on a first date about how busy they are. So often I'll get feedback from a client that the person I set them up with kept saying how busy they were—giving the other person a sense, probably correct, that they're too busy for love.

To which I say:

The world is busy! Get over yourself!

The Sad-Victim Dater

Everything about them says *feel sorry for me*. All conversations lead to their victimhood: a bad breakup, a painful divorce, a difficult childhood. Even when the Sad-Victim Dater isn't crossing over into being a Blamer or an Angry Dater, this type often fixates on emotional pain, which, while understandable and worthy of your compassion, can be a total turnoff on a date. People should be getting to know each other on first and second dates, not dumping their entire depressing life story and oversharing to the point of telling someone they hardly know way too much information about themselves and their unfortunate past. There's a time and a place to share things of this nature and it's usually sometime after the third date—assuming the Sad-Victim Dater can make it that far.

The Shallow Dater

The Shallow Dater always looks for the most attractive women or men to date. And the Shallow Dater always ends up with the most narcissistic women or men. I had a man in my new office in Michigan who was very handsome and told me he only wanted to meet brunettes. I said, "But you're in Michigan where there are so many beautiful Swedes! Get over yourself!" Shallow Daters are almost always narcissistic people themselves; they have low self-esteem and their shaky self-worth is increased by attractive dates.

The Show-Off

The Show-Off can be either male or female. Both are braggers and boasters—always talking about what they own and how much money they're worth. Show-Offs are turnoffs who need to stop talking about what they have and start thinking about what they *don't* have: love.

The Shy Dater

For the Shy Dater, the biggest obstacle is usually starting conversations, keeping conversations going, and getting past the first twenty minutes of a date. Being shy isn't such a bad thing—and more pleasant than it isn't, in fact—so women should cut shy guys a little slack and give them a chance to get their footing. The over-thirty-five shy man is more likely to be successful because the women he's dating have reached a place where they're less narrow-minded and more accepting, and they won't automatically disqualify a guy for not being a perfect conversationalist.

Because most Shy Daters aren't deeply troubled at their core, with a little coaching and some tips on topics to talk about and topics to steer clear of and a lot of practice with friends—and with a little chemistry with their date—the Shy Dater can almost always become a successful dater.

The Slob

Women complain a lot about men being slobs—which they sometimes are—but women are guilty of this, too. Male or female, a slob is a slob, either in the way they dress (sloppy), or eat (sloppily), or keep house (a giant slopfest). True Slobs are the ones consistently and disgustingly sloppy in all three areas, which, not surprisingly, makes them extremely difficult to match and to coach through a first date. One of the things I tell my clients who fit this type is: *Even if you're a slob, fake it.* Managed to get to the second or third date with someone you really like? Better clean your house before you even think of bringing anyone back there. And if there's a chance you're going to drive them anywhere, how about getting the fast-food bags out of the car? (You'd be amazed at how many people forget to clean out their cars when they're cleaning up their act.) But if they're willing to clean house—literally and figuratively—Slobs can almost always become very successful daters.

The Sports Junkie

This type of dater—almost always male—flies in under the radar as a problem type, because at first glance what's more normal and natural than a guy who's into sports? But the extreme version of the Sports Junkie crosses a line into obsessive behavior and even voyeurism. Sports Junkies are tolerated very early on by the women they date because "real guys" watch sports, yet sometimes their obsession with football and baseball and basketball takes over and completely dominates their relationships to the point of "widowing" the women who are involved with them. A tendency toward open and flagrant homophobia is often also a trait of the Sports Junkie. This type of Sports Junkie almost always has deep-rooted issues—demons they often don't even know about—that are easily masked by this type of marginally acceptable behavior. Garden-variety Sports Junkies can be coached to understand that they have to adjust their priorities—human contact and interaction first, watching sports second—but the truly addicted Sports Junkies are more resistant to change or behavior modification.

The Tough Girl

The Tough Girl is a younger and less refined version of the Classic Bitch. Unsophisticated, unladylike, and usually chewing gum, swearing, smoking, and drinking—often all at the same time—the Tough Girl can usually make great strides after a refresher course in table manners, general etiquette, and basic social skills.

The Uptight Dater

If it's a guy, he's the one in the bow tie and the argyle socks. If it's a woman, she's the one in a turtleneck or buttoned up in a suit straight from the office. When uptight daters come into my office I say this: *Relax. And lighten up.* Because if you don't, no one's ever going to feel comfortable enough around you for a second date.

THE LIST OF BEST POSSIBLE DATING TYPES: A VERY VERY SHORT LIST

The Positive Dater

Even if they're average-looking—*because the world is made up of average and that's okay!*—Positive Daters have a much better chance of being successful because they're willing to change and to try new things. A positive attitude—or the lack of it—can absolutely make or break dating and is the number one factor in whether you will be successful in your search for love. Because when you give good energy, you receive it.

Appendix 2

Patti's Mind-Body-Soul Healing Resources

DENTISTS

1-800-DENTIST

DIET AND WEIGHT LOSS

Weight Watchers
www.weightwatchers.com

FITNESS AND EXERCISE

Curves
http://www.curves.com

Bob Greene's The Best Life
www.thebestlife.com

GRIEF AND BEREAVEMENT

www.bereavedparentsusa.org

www.griefwatch.com

GENERAL HEALTH

www.health.com

You: The Owner's Manual (Dr. Roizen and Dr. Oz)
www.realage.com

MAKEUP AND COSMETICS

Mary Kay Cosmetics
www.marykaycosmetics.com

Avon Cosmetics
http://www.avon.com

Sephora
www.sephora.com

MONEY, FINANCE, AND BUDGETING

Suze Orman
www.suzeorman.com

National Foundation for Credit Counseling (800) 388-2227
Also known as Consumer Credit Counseling Service (CCCS)
www.nfcc.org

Debtors Anonymous
781-453-2743
www.debtorsanonymous.org

Smart Money
www.smartmoney.com
Tel: (202) 265-9572
Fax: (202) 328-9162

PLUS-SIZE CLOTHING

Lane Bryant
www.lanebryant.com

Nordstrom
http://shop.nordstrom.com

Macy's
www.macys.com

Bloomingdales
www.bloomingdales.com

Target
www.target.com

Big and Tall
www.bigandtall.com

SPIRITUALITY

www.beliefnet.com

SUBSTANCE ABUSE

Al-Anon
www.al-anon.alateen.org

THERAPY AND COUNSELING

American Psychological Association Help Center
www.apahelpcenter.org

Psychology Today Therapist Locator
http://therapists.psychologytoday.com

VOLUNTEERING AND DOING GOOD

www.1-800-volunteer.org

American Cancer Society
www.cancer.org

American Red Cross
www.redcross.org

The American Society for the Prevention of Cruelty to Animals
www.aspca.org

Big Brothers Big Sisters
www.bbbs.org

Camp Good Days and Special Times
www.campgooddays.org

Catholic Charities USA
www.catholiccharitiesusa.org

Epilepsy Foundation
www.epilepsyfoundation.org

Habitat for Humanity
www.habitat.org

Oprah's Angel Network
www.oprahsangelnetwork.org

People for the Ethical Treatment of Animals
www.peta.org

UNICEF
www.unicef.org

www.volunteermatch.org

Acknowledgments

To my daughter, Jessica, for her profound spirit and wisdom, who has helped raise me and who found Laura Zigman.

To Kurt, for the magic that came to me in my early 40s. I love you.

To Steve Novak for seeing me through some of my toughest times with my health, and with our daughter's as well.

To my father and mentor, James C. Lindner, for teaching me that hard work pays off, the squeaky wheel gets the oil, and that sympathy can be found between *shit* and *syphilis* in the dictionary. To my mother, Bobbie Lindner, who taught me to always see the half-empty glass of lemons as a half-full glass of lemonade.

To my brother and protector, Five-Job-Jimmy, who let the air out of my tires when I was ten, and to my sisters, Karen, Mary, and Jeannie, I love all of you.

To my chosen family—Nadine (Wetter) Greene, Joan Forster, Nora Cleary, Terri VanDuzer, Sandi Lachut, and Dayna Mecca—the best friends I could ever ask for.

To Laura Zigman, for her undeniable talent and good energy.

To Ballantine and Random House.

To all my brave clients who've shared their lives, world, and wisdom with me.

Last but not least—to the angels above for being my conscience and accompanying me on this journey.

ABOUT THE AUTHORS

PATTI NOVAK was the star of the critically acclaimed A&E series *Confessions of a Matchmaker.* She has appeared widely on television, including on *The Oprah Winfrey Show, The Rachael Ray Show,* and *The Early Show,* and has been featured in *The New York Times, The Wall Street Journal,* and *The New York Observer,* among other publications. She lives in Buffalo, New York, where she was born and raised, and where her matchmaking business, Buffalo Niagara Introductions, is based.

LAURA ZIGMAN is the author of four novels, the *New York Times* bestselling *Animal Husbandry,* which was made into the movie *Someone Like You, Dating Big Bird, Her,* and *Piece of Work.* She has written for *The New York Times, The Washington Post,* and *USA Today,* among other publications, and is a contributor to The Huffington Post. A longtime chronicler of the dating world, she lives outside Boston with her husband and young son.

ABOUT THE TYPE

This book was set in Sabon, a typeface designed by the well-known German typographer Jan Tschichold (1902–74). Sabon's design is based upon the original letter forms of Claude Garamond and was created specifically to be used for three sources: foundry type for hand composition, Linotype, and Monotype. Tschichold named his typeface for the famous Frankfurt typefounder Jacques Sabon, who died in 1580.